CHARTBOOK

A REFERENCE GRAMMAR

UNDERSTANDING AND USING English Grammar

FIFTH EDITION

Betty S. Azar
Stacy A. Hagen

Understanding and Using English Grammar, Fifth Edition Chartbook

Copyright ©2017, 2010, 2000, 1993, by Betty Schrampfer Azar
All rights reserved.

Pearson Education, 221 River Street, Hoboken, NJ 07030

Staff credits: The people who made up the *Understanding and Using English Grammar, Fifth Edition Chartbook* team, representing content creation, design, manufacturing, project management, and publishing, are Pietro Alongi, Rhea Banker, Stephanie Bullard, Tracey Cataldo, Warren Fischbach, Nancy Flaggman, Gosia Jaros-White, Brian Panker, Robert Ruvo, and Paula Van Ells.

Composition: Aptara
Contributing Editor: Janice L. Baillie

Illustrations: Don Martinetti, pages 8, 12, 15, 28, 36, 54, 96, 115, 119, 120, 123; Chris Pavely, pages 4, 13, 18, 21, 35 (top), 72, 101

Photos: Page 1: Cameraman/Fotolia; 2 (bottom, left): Dmitry Vereshchagin/Fotolia; 2 (bottom, right): Marc Xavier/Fotolia; 2 (top, center): WavebreakmediaMicro/Fotolia; 2 (top, left): WavebreakmediaMicro/Fotolia; 2 (top, right): Twin Design/Shutterstock; 5: Patryk Kosmider/Fotolia; 6: Jstaley4011/Fotolia; 7: Freesurf/Fotolia; 10: Fotomaximum/Fotolia; 22: Monkey Business/Fotolia; 26: Aiisha/Fotolia; 34: Mariusz Blach/Fotolia; 35 (bottom): Harris Shiffman/Fotolia; 37 (top): Ingusk/Fotolia; 38: Wabkmiami/Fotolia; 47: Chagin/Fotolia; 55: BlueSkyImages/Fotolia; 59: Halfpoint/Fotolia; 61: VIPDesign/Fotolia; 62: George Spade/Fotolia; 69: Jenifoto/Fotolia; 77: Pavel Kirichenko/Fotolia; 82: Richard Griffin/Fotolia; 84: Richard Griffin/Fotolia; 86: Hansenn/Fotolia; 103: Rtimages/Fotolia; 105: Focus Pocus LTD/Fotolia; 106: Timothy Masters/Fotolia

Printed in the United States of America
ISBN 10: 0-13-427628-0
ISBN 13: 978-0-13-427628-1

4 2020

Contents

Preface to the Fifth Edition viii

Chapter 1 PRESENT AND PAST; SIMPLE AND PROGRESSIVE 1

1-1 Simple Present and Present Progressive 1
1-2 Simple Present and Present Progressive: Affirmative,
     Negative, Question Forms 2
1-3 Verbs Not Usually Used in the Progressive (Stative Verbs) 3
1-4 Simple Past Tense 4
1-5 Simple Past vs. Past Progressive 5
1-6 Unfulfilled Intentions: *Was/Were Going To*. 6

Chapter 2 PERFECT AND PERFECT PROGRESSIVE TENSES .7

2-1   Regular and Irregular Verbs 7
2-2   Irregular Verb List 8
2-3   Present Perfect: *Since* and *For* 10
2-4   Present Perfect: Unspecified Time and Repeated Events 11
2-5   *Have* and *Has* in Spoken English 12
2-6   Present Perfect vs. Simple Past 13
2-7   Present Perfect Progressive 14
2-8   Past Perfect 15
2-9   *Had* in Spoken English 16
2-10 Past Perfect Progressive 16

Chapter 3 FUTURE TIME 17

3-1 Simple Future: Forms of *Will* and *Be Going To* 17
3-2 *Will* vs. *Be Going To* 18
3-3 Expressing the Future in Time Clauses 19
3-4 Using the Present Progressive and the Simple Present to
     Express Future Time 19
3-5 Future Progressive 20
3-6 Future Perfect and Future Perfect Progressive 20

Chapter 4 REVIEW OF VERB TENSES 21

Chapter 5 SUBJECT-VERB AGREEMENT 22

5-1 Final *-s/-es:* Use and Spelling 22
5-2 Basic Subject-Verb Agreement 23
5-3 Collective Nouns 23
5-4 Subject-Verb Agreement: Using Expressions of Quantity 24

| | 5-5 | Subject-Verb Agreement: Using *There* + *Be* . . . . | 24 |
| | 5-6 | Subject-Verb Agreement: Some Irregularities . . . . | 25 |

Chapter 6 NOUNS 26

	6-1	Regular and Irregular Plural Nouns	27
	6-2	Nouns as Adjectives	28
	6-3	Possessive Nouns	28
	6-4	More About Expressing Possession	29
	6-5	Count and Noncount Nouns	29
	6-6	Noncount Nouns	30
	6-7	Some Common Noncount Nouns	30
	6-8	Expressions of Quantity Used with Count and Noncount Nouns	31
	6-9	Using *A Few* and *Few*; *A Little* and *Little*	31
	6-10	Singular Expressions of Quantity: *One, Each, Every*	32
	6-11	Using *Of* in Expressions of Quantity	32

Chapter 7 ARTICLES 33

	7-1	Articles (*A, An, The*) with Indefinite and Definite Nouns	33
	7-2	Articles: Generic Nouns	34
	7-3	Descriptive Information with Definite and Indefinite Nouns	35
	7-4	General Guidelines for Article Usage	36
	7-5	Using *The* or Ø with Titles and Geographic Names	37

Chapter 8 PRONOUNS 38

	8-1	Pronouns and Possessive Adjectives	39
	8-2	Agreement with Generic Nouns and Indefinite Pronouns	40
	8-3	Personal Pronouns: Agreement with Collective Nouns	40
	8-4	Reflexive Pronouns	41
	8-5	Using *You*, *One*, and *They* as Impersonal Pronouns	41
	8-6	Forms of *Other*	42
	8-7	Common Expressions with *Other*	43

Chapter 9 MODALS, PART 1 44

	9-1	Basic Modal Introduction	44
	9-2	Expressing Necessity: *Must, Have To, Have Got To*	45
	9-3	Lack of Necessity (*Not Have To*) and Prohibition (*Must Not*)	45
	9-4	Advisability/Suggestions: *Should, Ought To, Had Better, Could*	46
	9-5	Expectation: *Be Supposed To/Should*	47
	9-6	Ability: *Can, Know How To*, and *Be Able To*	48
	9-7	Possibility: *Can, May, Might*	48
	9-8	Requests and Responses with Modals	49
	9-9	Polite Requests with *Would You Mind*	50
	9-10	Making Suggestions: *Let's, Why Don't, Shall I /We*	50

Chapter 10 MODALS, PART 2 51

	10-1	Using *Would* to Express a Repeated Action in the Past	51
	10-2	Expressing the Past: Necessity, Advice, Expectation	51
	10-3	Expressing Past Ability	52
	10-4	Degrees of Certainty: Present Time	52
	10-5	Degrees of Certainty: Present Time Negative	53

10-6   Degrees of Certainty: Past Time 53
10-7   Degrees of Certainty: Future Time 54
10-8   Progressive Forms of Modals 54
10-9   Combining Modals with Phrasal Modals 55
10-10 Expressing Preference: *Would Rather* 55
10-11 Summary Chart of Modals and Similar Expressions 56

Chapter 11   THE PASSIVE **58**
11-1   Active vs. Passive 58
11-2   Tense Forms of the Passive 58
11-3   Using the Passive 59
11-4   The Passive Form of Modals and Phrasal Modals 59
11-5   Stative (Non-Progressive) Passive 60
11-6   Common Stative (Non-Progressive) Passive Verbs + Prepositions 60
11-7   The Passive with *Get* 61
11-8   *-ed/-ing* Adjectives 62

Chapter 12   NOUN CLAUSES **63**
12-1   Introduction 63
12-2   Noun Clauses with Question Words 64
12-3   Noun Clauses with *Whether* or *If* 64
12-4   Question Words Followed by Infinitives 65
12-5   Noun Clauses with *That* 65
12-6   Quoted Speech 66
12-7   Reported Speech 67
12-8   Reported Speech: Modal Verbs in Noun Clauses 68
12-9   The Subjunctive in Noun Clauses 68

Chapter 13   ADJECTIVE CLAUSES **69**
13-1   Adjective Clause Pronouns Used as the Subject 69
13-2   Adjective Clause Pronouns Used as the Object of a Verb 70
13-3   Adjective Clause Pronouns Used as the Object of a Preposition 70
13-4   Using *Whose* 71
13-5   Using *Where* in Adjective Clauses 71
13-6   Using *When* in Adjective Clauses 71
13-7   Using Adjective Clauses to Modify Pronouns 72
13-8   Punctuating Adjective Clauses 73
13-9   Using Expressions of Quantity in Adjective Clauses 73
13-10 Using *Which* to Modify a Whole Sentence 74
13-11 Reducing Adjective Clauses to Adjective Phrases 74

Chapter 14   GERUNDS AND INFINITIVES, PART 1 . . . . **75**
14-1   Gerunds and Infinitives: Introduction 75
14-2   Common Verbs Followed by Gerunds 75
14-3   Common Verbs Followed by Infinitives 76
14-4   Infinitives with Objects 76
14-5   Common Verbs Followed by Either Infinitives or Gerunds 77
14-6   Using Gerunds as the Objects of Prepositions 78
14-7   *Go* + Gerund 78
14-8   Special Expressions Followed by *-ing* 79
14-9   *It* + Infinitive; Gerunds and Infinitives as Subjects 79

14-10 Reference List of Verbs Followed by Infinitives 80
14-11 Reference List of Verbs Followed by Gerunds 81
14-12 Reference List of Preposition Combinations Followed by Gerunds. 82

Chapter 15   GERUNDS AND INFINITIVES, PART 2 83
15-1   Infinitive of Purpose: *In Order To* 83
15-2   Adjectives Followed by Infinitives 83
15-3   Using Infinitives with *Too* and *Enough* 84
15-4   Passive Infinitives and Gerunds: Present 84
15-5   Past Forms of Infinitives and Gerunds: Active and Passive 85
15-6   Using Gerunds or Passive Infinitives Following *Need* 85
15-7   Using Verbs of Perception 86
15-8   Using the Simple Form After *Let* and *Help* 86
15-9   Using Causative Verbs: *Make, Have, Get* 87
15-10 Using a Possessive to Modify a Gerund 87

Chapter 16   COORDINATING CONJUNCTIONS 88
16-1   Parallel Structure 88
16-2   Parallel Structure: Using Commas 88
16-3   Punctuation for Independent Clauses; Connecting
       Them with *And* and *But* 89
16-4   Paired Conjunctions: *Both … And; Not Only … But Also;*
       Either … Or; Neither … Nor 89

Chapter 17   ADVERB CLAUSES 90
17-1   Introduction 90
17-2   Using Adverb Clauses to Show Time Relationships 91
17-3   Using Adverb Clauses to Show Cause and Effect 92
17-4   Expressing Contrast (Unexpected Result): Using *Even Though* 92
17-5   Showing Direct Contrast: *While* 92
17-6   Expressing Conditions in Adverb Clauses: *If*-Clauses 93
17-7   Shortened *If*-Clauses 93
17-8   Adverb Clauses of Condition: Using *Whether Or Not* and *Even If* 93
17-9   Adverb Clauses of Condition: Using *In Case* 94
17-10 Adverb Clauses of Condition: Using *Unless* 94
17-11 Adverb Clauses of Condition: Using *Only If* 94

Chapter 18   REDUCTION OF ADVERB CLAUSES TO MODIFYING
ADVERBIAL PHRASES 95
18-1   Introduction 95
18-2   Changing Time Clauses to Modifying Adverbial Phrases 96
18-3   Expressing the Idea of "During the Same Time" in
       Modifying Adverbial Phrases 96
18-4   Expressing Cause and Effect in Modifying Adverbial Phrases 97
18-5   Using *Upon* + *-ing* in Modifying Adverbial Phrases 97

Chapter 19   CONNECTIVES THAT EXPRESS CAUSE AND EFFECT,
CONTRAST, AND CONDITION 98
19-1   Introduction. 98
19-2   Using *Because Of* and *Due To* 99
19-3   Cause and Effect: Using *Therefore, Consequently*, and *So*. 99

19-4   Summary of Patterns and Punctuation 100

19-5   Other Ways of Expressing Cause and Effect:
Such ... That and *So ... That* 100

19-6   Expressing Purpose: Using *So That* 101

19-7   Showing Contrast (Unexpected Result) 102

19-8   Showing Direct Contrast 102

19-9   Expressing Conditions: Using *Otherwise* and *Or (Else)* 103

Chapter 20   CONDITIONAL SENTENCES AND WISHES **104**

20-1   Overview of Basic Verb Forms Used in Conditional Sentences 104

20-2   Expressing Real Conditions in the Present or Future 104

20-3   Unreal (Contrary to Fact) in the Present or Future 105

20-4   Unreal (Contrary to Fact) in the Past 105

20-5   Using Progressive Verb Forms in Conditional Sentences 106

20-6   Using "Mixed Time" in Conditional Sentences 106

20-7   Omitting *If* 106

20-8   Implied Conditions 107

20-9   Wishes About the Present and Past 107

20-10 Wishes About the Future; Use of *Wish + Would* 107

Appendix   SUPPLEMENTARY GRAMMAR CHARTS **108**

Unit A: **Basic Grammar Terminology** 108

A-1   Subjects, Verbs, and Objects 108

A-2   Adjectives 108

A-3   Adverbs 109

A-4   Prepositions and Prepositional Phrases 109

A-5   Preposition Combinations with Adjectives and Verbs 110

Unit B: **Questions** 111

B-1   Forms of *Yes/No* and Information Questions 111

B-2   Question Words 112

B-3   Shortened *Yes/No* Questions 114

B-4   Negative Questions 114

B-5   Tag Questions 115

Unit C: **Contractions** 116

Unit D: **Negatives** 117

D-1   Using *Not* and Other Negative Words 117

D-2   Avoiding Double Negatives 117

D-3   Beginning a Sentence with a Negative Word 117

Unit E: **Verbs** 118

E-1   The Verb *Be* 118

E-2   Spelling of *-ing* and *-ed* Verb Forms 118

E-3   Overview of Verb Tenses 119

E-4   Summary of Verb Tenses 121

E-5   Regular Verbs: Pronunciation of *-ed* Endings 122

E-6   Pronunciation of Final *-s* in Verbs and Nouns 122

E-7   Linking Verbs 123

E-8   Troublesome Verbs: *Raise/Rise, Set/Sit, Lay/Lie* 123

E-9   Irregular Verbs: An Alphabetical Reference List 124

Index **127**

Preface

Understanding and Using English Grammar Chartbook is a grammar reference for English language learners. It contains all the charts found in the student text *Understanding and Using English Grammar, fifth edition.* The information that English language learners want and need in order to communicate effectively is presented clearly, accurately, and concisely.

Intended as a reference tool for students and teachers alike, the *Chartbook* can be used alone or in conjunction with the *Workbook.* The practices in the *Workbook* are keyed to the charts in the *Chartbook.* Since the *Workbook* provides answers to all the practices, a *Chartbook* plus *Workbook* combination allows learners to study independently. More advanced students can work through much of the grammar on their own. They can investigate and correct their usage problems, expand their usage repertoire by doing self-study practices in the *Workbook*, and find answers to most of their grammar questions in the Chartbook.

Teachers and students may find the *Chartbook* plus *Workbook* combination especially useful in writing classes, in tutorials, or in rapid reviews in which grammar is not the main focus but needs attention.

The *Teacher's Guide* contains background teaching notes for all the charts, as well as step-by-step instructions for in-class use. In addition, there are beyond-the-book *PowerPoint* lessons in MyEnglishLab, Essential Online Resources, and AzarGrammar.com, which highlight several key grammar structures.

Present and Past;
Simple and Progressive

1-1 Simple Present and Present Progressive

This basic diagram will be used in all tense descriptions.

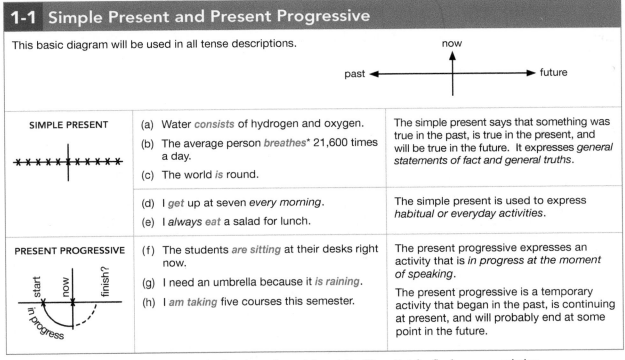

SIMPLE PRESENT	(a) Water *consists* of hydrogen and oxygen.	The simple present says that something was true in the past, is true in the present, and will be true in the future. It expresses *general statements of fact and general truths*.
	(b) The average person *breathes** 21,600 times a day.	
	(c) The world *is* round.	
	(d) I *get* up at seven *every morning*.	The simple present is used to express *habitual or everyday activities*.
	(e) I *always eat* a salad for lunch.	
PRESENT PROGRESSIVE	(f) The students *are sitting* at their desks right now.	The present progressive expresses an activity that is *in progress at the moment of speaking*.
	(g) I need an umbrella because it *is raining*.	The present progressive is a temporary activity that began in the past, is continuing at present, and will probably end at some point in the future.
	(h) I *am taking* five courses this semester.	

*See Appendix Chart E-2 for spelling rules for *-ing* verbs and Appendix Chart E-6 for final *-s* pronunciation.

Our galaxy *contains* from 100 to 400 billion stars.

	Simple Present			Present Progressive		
AFFIRMATIVE	I	*help.*		I	*am*	*helping.*
	You, We, They	*help.*		You, We, They	*are*	*helping.*
	He, She, It	*helps.*		He, She, It	*is*	*helping.*
NEGATIVE	I	*do not*	*help.*	I	*am not*	*helping.*
	You, We, They	*do not*	*help.*	You, We, They	*are not*	*helping.*
	He, She, It	*does not*	*help.*	He, She, It	*is not*	*helping.*
QUESTION	*Do*	I	*help?*	*Am*	I	*helping?*
	Do	you, we, they	*help?*	*Are*	you, we, they	*helping?*
	Does	he, she, it	*help?*	*Is*	he, she, it	*helping?*
	When do	I	*help?*	*When am*	I	*helping?*

These drivers *are* probably *breaking* the law. The men *are using* their phones. The women *are not using* their phones, but they *are not paying* attention. *What do* you *think* of their driving habits?

1-3 Verbs Not Usually Used in the Progressive (Stative Verbs)

(a) I *know* your cousin. (b) INCORRECT: I ~~am knowing~~ your cousin.	Some verbs, like **know**, are *stative* or *non-progressive*. They describe states, not actions, and are rarely used in progressive tenses. ("States" are conditions or situations that exist.)

Common Verbs That Are Usually Non-Progressive (like *know*)

know	like	dislike	belong	consist of	hear	agree
believe	appreciate	fear	possess	contain	sound	disagree
doubt	care about	hate	own			mean
recognize	please	mind		exist	seem	promise
remember	prefer		desire	matter	look like	amaze
suppose			need		resemble	surprise
understand			want			
			wish			

(c) I *think* that your cousin is very nice. (d) I'*m thinking* about my trip to Rome.	Some verbs, like **think**, have both *non-progressive* meanings and *progressive* meanings. In (c): **think** means "believe." In (d): **am thinking** means "thoughts are going around in my mind right now."

Common Verbs with Both Non-Progressive and Progressive Meanings (like *think*)

	NON-PROGRESSIVE	PROGRESSIVE
look	It *looks* cold outside.	Olga *is looking* out the window.
appear	Jack *appears* to be tired today.	She'*s appearing* on a TV show today.
think	I *think* that Mr. Liu is a good teacher.	I'*m thinking* about my family right now.
feel	I *feel* that Mr. Liu is a good teacher.	I'*m feeling* a little tired today.
have	I *have* a bike.	I'*m having* a good time.
see	*Do* you *see* that bird?	The doctor *is seeing* a patient right now.
taste	The soup *tastes* salty.	The chef *is tasting* the soup.
smell	Something *smells* bad. What is it?	Ann *is smelling* the perfume to see if she wants to buy it.
love	Ken *loves* his baby daughter.	Ken is enjoying parenthood. In fact, he'*s loving* it!
be	Mary *is* old and wise.	Al is ill but won't see a doctor. He *is being foolish*.*

*__*Am/is/are being__* + *an adjective* describes temporary behavior. In the example, Al is usually not foolish, but right now he is acting that way.

1-4 Simple Past Tense

(a) It *snowed** yesterday. (b) Tom *watched* TV last night.	*At one particular time in the past,* this happened. It began and ended in the past. Most simple past verbs add *-ed*, as in (a) and (b).
(c) Jack *went* to work early. (d) I *came* to work late. (e) We *saw* a great movie last night.	Some verbs have irregular past tense forms, as in (c), (d), and (e). NOTE: See Appendix Chart E-9 for a list of irregular verb forms.
(f) Emily *was* at the office this morning. (g) You *were* tired yesterday.	The simple past forms of **be** are **was** and **were**, as in (f) and (g).
(h) Andrew *caught* the ball, *ran* down the field, and *scored* a point.	Note that in a series of actions, the verbs are the same tense, as in (h). INCORRECT: Andrew caught the ball, ~~is running~~ down the field, and ~~score~~ a point.

Regular Verb Forms

AFFIRMATIVE	NEGATIVE	QUESTION
I You He, She, It } *helped.* We They	I You He, She, It } *did not help.* We They	*Did* I *Did* you *Did* he, she, it } *help?* *Did* we *Did* they

Irregular Verb Forms

AFFIRMATIVE	NEGATIVE	QUESTION
I You He, She, It } *ate.* We They	I You He, She, It } *did not eat.* We They	*Did* I *Did* you *Did* he, she, it } *eat?* *Did* we *Did* they

Be Verb Forms

AFFIRMATIVE			NEGATIVE			QUESTION		
I, He, She, It	*was*	here.	I, He, She, It	*was not*	here.	*Was*	I, he, she, it	here?
You, We, They	*were*	here.	You, We, They	*were not*	here.	*Were*	you, we, they	here?

*See Appendix Chart E-5 for information about final *-ed* pronunciation.

1-5 Simple Past vs. Past Progressive

SIMPLE PAST		
(a) I *walked* to school yesterday. (b) John *lived* in Paris for ten years, but now he lives in Rome. (c) I *bought* a new car three days ago.	The simple past indicates that an activity or situation *began and ended at a particular time in the past.*
(d) Rita *stood* under a tree *when it began* to rain. (e) *When Mrs. Chu heard a strange noise,* she *got* up to investigate. (f) *When I dropped my cup,* the coffee *spilled* on my lap.	If a sentence contains **when** and has the simple past in both clauses, the action in the *when*-clause happens first. In (d): 1st: The rain began. 2nd: Rita stood under a tree.
PAST PROGRESSIVE		
(g) I *was walking* down the street when it began to rain. (h) While I *was walking* down the street, it began to rain. (i) Rita *was standing* under a tree when it began to rain. (j) At eight o'clock last night, I *was studying.*	In (g): 1st: I was walking down the street. 2nd: It began to rain. Both actions occurred at the same time, but *one action began earlier and was in progress when the other action occurred.* In (j): My studying began before 8:00, was in progress at that time, and probably continued.
(k) While I *was studying* in one room of our apartment, my roommate *was having* a party in the other room.	Sometimes the past progressive is used in both parts of a sentence when two actions are in progress simultaneously.

Nan *was thinking* about a vacation *when* her son **brought** home a travel brochure. The family **decided** to go to a Greek island.

1-6 Unfulfilled Intentions: *Was / Were Going To*

(a) Jack *was going to go* to the movie last night, but he changed his mind.	*Was / were going to* talk about past intentions. Usually, these are unfulfilled intentions, i.e., activities someone intended to do but did not do. The meaning in (a): *Jack was planning to go to the movie, but he didn't go.*
(b) I *was planning* to go, but I didn't. I *was hoping* to go, but I couldn't. I *was intending* to go, but I didn't. I *was thinking about* going, but I didn't.	Other ways of expressing unfulfilled intentions are to use *plan, hope, intend,* and *think about* in the past progressive, as in (b).

The Carters *were going to go* to the park, but they didn't. They stayed home and gave their dog a bath!

CHAPTER 2

Perfect and Perfect Progressive Tenses

2-1 Regular and Irregular Verbs

Regular Verbs: The simple past and past participle end in *-ed.*

SIMPLE FORM	SIMPLE PAST	PAST PARTICIPLE	PRESENT PARTICIPLE
hope	hoped	hoped	hoping
stop	stopped	stopped	stopping
listen	listened	listened	listening
study	studied	studied	studying
start	started	started	starting

English verbs have four principal parts:
(1) simple form
(2) simple past
(3) past participle
(4) present participle

Irregular Verbs: The simple past and past participle do not end in *-ed.*

SIMPLE FORM	SIMPLE PAST	PAST PARTICIPLE	PRESENT PARTICIPLE
hit	hit	hit	hitting
find	found	found	finding
swim	swam	swum	swimming
break	broke	broken	breaking
wear	wore	worn	wearing

Some verbs have irregular past forms.

Most of the irregular verbs in English are given in the alphabetical list in Appendix Chart E-9.

In ancient times, people *drew* pictures and *wrote* on papyrus, parchment, and later, paper. They *used* various natural substances to make ink.

2-2 Irregular Verb List

Group 1: All three forms are the same.

SIMPLE FORM	SIMPLE PAST	PAST PARTICIPLE	SIMPLE FORM	SIMPLE PAST	PAST PARTICIPLE
bet	bet	bet	let	let	let
burst	burst	burst	put	put	put
cost	cost	cost	quit*	quit	quit
cut	cut	cut	shut	shut	shut
fit	fit/fitted	fit/fitted	spread	spread	spread
hit	hit	hit	split	split	split
hurt	hurt	hurt	upset	upset	upset

*Also possible in BrE: *quit-quitted-quitted.*

Group 2: Past participle ends in -*en*.

bite	bit	bitten	hide	hid	hidden
break	broke	broken	mistake	mistook	mistaken
choose	chose	chosen	ride	rode	ridden
drive	drove	driven	rise	rose	risen
eat	ate	eaten	shake	shook	shaken
fall	fell	fallen	speak	spoke	spoken
forget	forgot	forgotten	steal	stole	stolen
forgive	forgave	forgiven	swell	swelled	swollen/swelled
freeze	froze	frozen	take	took	taken
get	got	gotten/got*	wake	woke	woken
give	gave	given	write	wrote	written

*In BrE: *get-got-got.* In AmE: *get-got-gotten/got.*

Group 3: Vowel changes from *a* in the simple past to *u* in the past participle.

begin	began	begun	sing	sang	sung
drink	drank	drunk	sink	sank	sunk
ring	rang	rung	stink	stank/stunk	stunk
run	ran	run	swim	swam	swum
shrink	shrank	shrunk			

The chef **put** too much salt in the sauce.
He **had forgotten** the recipe.

Group 4: Past tense and past participle forms are the same.

bend	bent	bent	mean	meant	meant
bleed	bled	bled	meet	met	met
bring	brought	brought	pay	paid	paid
build	built	built	read	read	read
buy	bought	bought	say	said	said
catch	caught	caught	sell	sold	sold
dig	dug	dug	send	sent	sent
feed	fed	fed	shoot	shot	shot
feel	felt	felt	sit	sat	sat
fight	fought	fought	sleep	slept	slept
find	found	found	slide	slid	slid
grind	ground	ground	sneak	snuck/sneaked	snuck/sneaked
hang*	hung	hung	speed	sped	sped
have	had	had	spend	spent	spent
hear	heard	heard	spin	spun	spun
hold	held	held	stand	stood	stood
keep	kept	kept	stick	stuck	stuck
lay	laid	laid	sting	stung	stung
lead	led	led	strike	struck	struck
leave	left	left	sweep	swept	swept
lend	lent	lent	swing	swung	swung
light	lit/lighted	lit/lighted	teach	taught	taught
lose	lost	lost	tell	told	told
make	made	made	think	thought	thought
			understand	understood	understood
			weep	wept	wept
			win	won	won

*__Hang__ is a regular verb when it means "to kill someone with a rope around his/her neck." COMPARE: *I hung my clothes in the closet. They* **hanged** *the murderer by the neck until he was dead.*

Group 5: Past participle adds final -*n* to the simple past, with or without a spelling change.

blow	blew	blown	see	saw	seen
do	did	done	swear	swore	sworn
draw	drew	drawn	tear	tore	torn
fly	flew	flown	throw	threw	thrown
grow	grew	grown	wear	wore	worn
know	knew	known	withdraw	withdrew	withdrawn
lie	lay	lain			

Group 6: The first and third forms are the same.

become	became	become
come	came	come
run	ran	run

Group 7: One of the three forms is very different.

be	was, were	been
go	went	gone

Group 8: Both regular and irregular forms are used. (The regular form is more common in AmE, and the irregular form is more common in BrE.)

awake	awakened/awoke	awakened/awoken	prove	proved/proven	proved/proven
burn	burned/burnt	burned/burnt	shine	shined/shone	shined/shone
dream	dreamed/dreamt	dreamed/dreamt	smell	smelled/smelt	smelled/smelt
kneel	kneeled/knelt	kneeled/knelt	spill	spilled/spilt	spilled/spilt
lean	leaned/leant	leaned/leant	spoil	spoiled/spoilt	spoiled/spoilt
learn	learned/learnt	learned/learn			

2-3 Present Perfect: *Since* and *For*

 2002 now up to now →	(a) Mrs. Oh *has been* a teacher *since* 2002.	The PRESENT PERFECT is often used with *since* and *for* to talk about *situations that began in the past and continue up to now.* PRESENT PERFECT FORM = *has/have* + past participle In (a): SITUATION = being a teacher TIME FRAME = from 2002 up to now
(b) I *have been* in this city *since* last May. (c) We *have been* here *since* nine o'clock. (d) Rita knows Rob. They met two months ago. She *has known* him *for* two months. I met him three years ago. I *have known* him *for* three years.		Notice the use of *since* vs. *for* in the examples: ***since*** + *a specific point in time* (e.g., *2002, last May, nine o'clock*) ***for*** + *a length of time* (e.g., *two months, three years*)
(e) I *have known* Rob *since I was in high school.* (f) We *have lived* in an apartment *since we moved to this city.*		A time clause (i.e., a subject and verb) may follow ***since***, as in (e) and (f).* NOTE: The verb before ***since*** is present perfect. The verb in the time clause is simple past.

*See Chart 17-2, p. 91, for more information about time clauses.

We *haven't swum* at that beach *since*
we *heard* about the sharks.

2-4 Present Perfect: Unspecified Time and Repeated Events

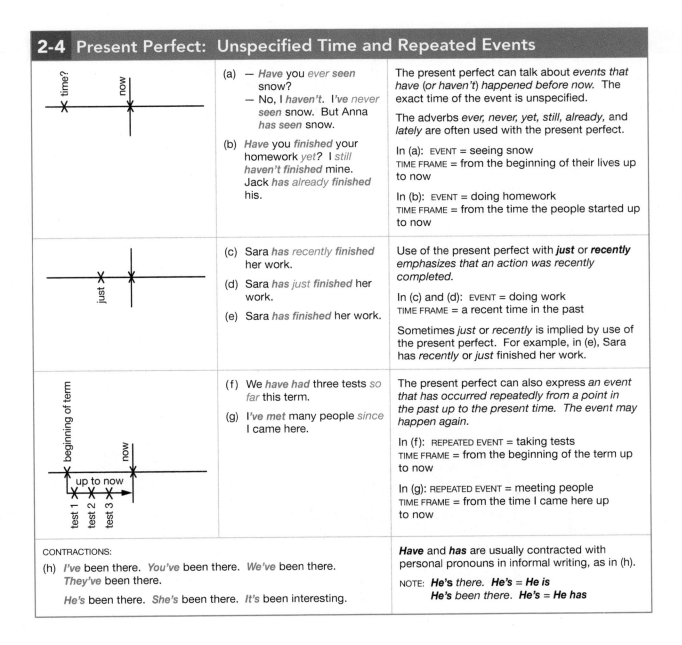

(a) — *Have* you *ever seen* snow?
— No, I *haven't.* I*'ve never seen* snow. But Anna *has seen* snow.

(b) *Have* you *finished* your homework *yet*? I *still haven't finished* mine. Jack *has already finished* his.

The present perfect can talk about *events that have (or haven't) happened before now.* The exact time of the event is unspecified.

The adverbs *ever, never, yet, still, already,* and *lately* are often used with the present perfect.

In (a): EVENT = seeing snow
TIME FRAME = from the beginning of their lives up to now

In (b): EVENT = doing homework
TIME FRAME = from the time the people started up to now

(c) Sara *has recently finished* her work.

(d) Sara *has just finished* her work.

(e) Sara *has finished* her work.

Use of the present perfect with *just* or *recently* emphasizes that an action was recently completed.

In (c) and (d): EVENT = doing work
TIME FRAME = a recent time in the past

Sometimes *just* or *recently* is implied by use of the present perfect. For example, in (e), Sara has *recently* or *just* finished her work.

(f) We *have had* three tests *so far* this term.

(g) I*'ve met* many people *since* I came here.

The present perfect can also express *an event that has occurred repeatedly from a point in the past up to the present time.* The event may happen again.

In (f): REPEATED EVENT = taking tests
TIME FRAME = from the beginning of the term up to now

In (g): REPEATED EVENT = meeting people
TIME FRAME = from the time I came here up to now

CONTRACTIONS:

(h) *I've* been there. *You've* been there. *We've* been there. *They've* been there.

He's been there. *She's* been there. *It's* been interesting.

Have and *has* are usually contracted with personal pronouns in informal writing, as in (h).

NOTE: *He's* there. *He's* = *He is*
He's been there. *He's* = *He has*

2-5 *Have* and *Has* in Spoken English

(a) **How have** you been?
 	
    Spoken: How/v/ you been? OR
             How/əv/ you been?
	In spoken English, the present perfect helping verbs **has** and **have** are often reduced following nouns and question words.*
	
	 In (a): **have** can sound like /v/ or /əv/.

(b) **Jane has** already eaten lunch.
 	
    Spoken: Jane/z/ already eaten lunch. OR
             Jane/əz/ already eaten lunch.
	In (b): **has** can sound like /z/ or /əz/.
	 In (c): **has** can sound like /s / or /əs/.**
	 NOTE: "ə" sounds like "uh."

(c) **Mike has** quit his job.
 	
    Spoken: Mike/s/ quit his job. OR
             Mike/əs/ quit his job.
	Jane/z/ eaten. **Jane's = Jane has**
	 Jane/z/ here. **Jane's = Jane is**
	
	 Mike/s/ quit his job. **Mike's = Mike has**
	 Mike/s/ here. **Mike's = Mike is**

*In very informal writing, **has** is sometimes contracted with nouns (e.g., **Jane's** *already eaten.*) and question words (e.g., **Where's** *he gone?*). **Have** is rarely contracted in writing except with pronouns (e.g., *I've*). See Chart 2-4 for written contractions of **have** and **has** with pronouns. See Appendix Chart C for more information about contractions in general.

See Appendix Chart E-6 for the pronunciation of final **-s after voiced and voiceless sounds.

Written: **Paul has** started too many projects. **He has** decided to rest for a while.

Spoken: *Paul /z/ (OR Paul/əz/) started too many projects.*

                 He /z/ decided to rest for a while.

2-6 Present Perfect vs. Simple Past

PRESENT PERFECT time? now	(a) I've *met* Linda, but I *haven't met* her husband. *Have* you *met* him?	The PRESENT PERFECT is used to talk about *past events when there is no specific mention of time.* In (a): The speaker is talking about *some unspecified time before now.*
SIMPLE PAST yesterday	(b) I *met* Helen *yesterday* at a party. Her husband *was* there too, but I *didn't meet* him. *Did* you *meet* him at the party?	The SIMPLE PAST is used when there is a *specific mention of time.* In (b): The speaker is thinking of a specific time: yesterday.
PRESENT PERFECT 10 years ago up to now	(c) Sam *has been* a math teacher *for* ten years. He loves teaching.	The PRESENT PERFECT is used for *situations that began in the past and continue to the present.* In (c): The present perfect tells us that Sam is still a teacher now.
SIMPLE PAST 2000–2010	(d) Jim *was* a teacher *for* ten years, from 2000 to 2010. Now he is an engineer.	The SIMPLE PAST is used for *situations that began and ended in the past.* In (d): The simple past tells us that Jim is not a teacher now.

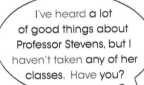

I've heard a lot of good things about Professor Stevens, but I haven't taken any of her classes. Have you?

Yes. I took one of her classes last year. I loved it.

2-7 Present Perfect Progressive

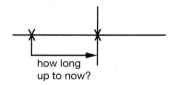

how long
up to now?

(a) Right now I **am sitting** at my desk.	COMPARE:
(b) I *have been sitting* at my desk *since* seven o'clock. *I have been sitting* here *for* two hours.	In (a): The PRESENT PROGRESSIVE expresses *an activity in progress right now.* (See Chart 1-1, p. 1.)
(c) It*'s been raining* all day. It*'s* still raining right now.	In (b): The PRESENT PERFECT PROGRESSIVE expresses *how long* an activity has been in progress. In other words, it expresses *the duration of an activity that began in the past and continues in the present.*
	Time expressions often used with this tense are • *since* and *for,* as in (b); • *all day/all morning/all week,* as in (c).
	NOTE: In (c): ***It's been raining. It's = It has*** ***It's still raining. It's = It is***
(d) I***'ve known*** Alex *since* he was a child. INCORRECT: ~~I've been knowing~~ Alex since he was a child.	The present perfect progressive is not used with non-progressive or stative verbs such as *know.* To express *the duration of a situation that began in the past and continues to the present,* only the present perfect is used. (See Chart 1-3, p. 3, for a list of non-progressive verbs.)
(e) How long *have* you *been living* here? (f) How long **have** you **lived** here? (g) Ben *has been wearing* glasses since he was ten. (h) Ben ***has worn*** glasses since he was ten.	For some (not all) verbs, the idea of *how long* can be expressed by either tense — the present perfect progressive or the present perfect. NOTE: (e) and (f) have the same meaning; (g) and (h) have the same meaning. Either tense can be used only when the verb expresses the duration of present activities or situations that happen regularly, usually, habitually: e.g., *live, work, teach, study, wear glasses, play chess,* etc.

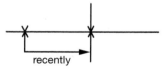

recently

(i) I*'ve been thinking* about looking for a different job. This one doesn't pay enough.	When the tense is used without any mention of time, it expresses a general activity in progress recently, lately. For example, (i) means *I've been thinking about this recently, lately.*
(j) All of the students *have been studying* hard. Final exams start next week.	

 /

	(a) Sam came at 10:00. Ann left at 9:30. In other words, Ann *had* already *left* when Sam came.	The PAST PERFECT expresses an *activity that was complete before another activity or time in the past.*

(b) *By the time* Sam came, Ann *had* already *left*.	In (a): 1st: Ann left. 2nd: Sam came. Adverb clauses with *by the time* are frequently used with the past perfect in the main clause, as in (b).*
(c) Sam *had left* before Ann came. (d) Sam *left* before Ann came. (e) *After* the guests *had left*, I went to bed. (f) *After* the guests *left*, I went to bed.	If either *before* or *after* is used in the sentence, the past perfect is often not necessary because the time relationship is already clear. The simple past may be used, as in (d) and (f). NOTE: (c) and (d) have the same meaning; (e) and (f) have the same meaning.
(g) *Actual spoken words*: I *lost* my keys. (h) *Reported words*: Jenny **said that** she *had lost* her keys.	The past perfect is commonly used in reported speech.** If the actual spoken words use the simple past, the past perfect is often used in reporting those words, as in (h). Common reporting verbs include *tell (someone), say, find out, learn,* and *discover.*
(i) *Written*: Bill *felt* great that evening. Earlier in the day, Annie *had caught* one fish, and he *had caught* three. They *had had* a delicious picnic near the lake and then *had gone* swimming again. It *had been* a nearly perfect vacation day.	The past perfect is often found in more formal writing such as fiction. In (i), the fiction writer uses the simple past to say that an event happened (*Bill felt great*), and then uses the past perfect to explain what had happened before that event.
(j) *I'd left. You'd left.* *We'd left. They'd left.* *She'd left. He'd left.* *It'd left.*	**Had** is often contracted with personal pronouns in informal writing. NOTE: **I'd left. I'd = I had** **I'd like to leave. I'd = I would**

*For more information about *by the time*, see Chart 17-2, p. 91.
**For more information about verb form usage in reported speech, see Chart 12-7, p. 67.

2-9 Had in Spoken English

(a) **Joe had** already heard the story. *Spoken:* Joe /d/ already heard the story. OR Joe /əd/ already heard the story. (b) **Who had** been there before you? *Spoken:* Who/d/ been there before you? OR Who/əd/ been there before you?	In spoken English, the helping verb **had** in the past perfect is often reduced following nouns and question words. It can be pronounced as /d/ or as /əd/.* NOTE: "ə" sounds like "uh."
(c) The dog **had** a bone. *Spoken:* The dog had a bone.	**Had** is not reduced when it is a main verb, as in (c).

*See Chart 2-8 for written contractions of **had** with pronouns.

2-10 Past Perfect Progressive

duration of waiting 4:30–6:00	(a) Eric finally came at six o'clock. I *had been waiting* for him *since* four-thirty. (b) The police *had been looking* for the criminal *for* two years before they caught him.	The PAST PERFECT PROGRESSIVE emphasizes the *duration of an activity that was in progress before another activity or time in the past.* NOTE: The past perfect progressive is used infrequently compared to other verb tenses.
close in time	(c) When Judy got home, her hair was still wet because she *had been swimming*. (d) I went to Ed's house after the funeral. His eyes were red because he *had been crying*.	This tense also may express an activity *in progress close in time to another activity or time in the past.*
(e) *Actual spoken words:* I *have been waiting* for you. (f) *Reported words:* Lia **told me that** she *had been waiting* for me.		The past perfect progressive also occurs in reported speech.

CHAPTER 3

Future Time

3-1 Simple Future: Forms of *Will* and *Be Going To*

(a) It *will* snow tomorrow. (b) It *is going to* snow tomorrow.	*Will* and *be going to* express future time and often have essentially the same meaning. Examples (a) and (b) have the same meaning. See Chart 3-2 for differences in meaning between the two forms.

Will

(c) The weather *will turn* cold tonight. INCORRECT: The weather wills-turn cold. INCORRECT: The weather will turns-cold. INCORRECT: The weather will to-turn cold.	*Will* typically expresses predictions about the future, as in (c). *Will* does not take a final *-s*. *Will* is followed immediately by the simple form of a verb.
(d) It *will not warm* up for several days. (e) The snow *won't melt* soon.	NEGATIVE: *will + not = won't*
(f) *Will* it be icy *tomorrow?* How *will you get* here?	QUESTION: *will + subject + main verb* In (e): The speaker is asking for information about a future event.*
(g) *Spoken* or *written:* It'll be cold. (h) *Spoken:* Tom'll shovel the snow. *Written:* Tom will shovel the snow. (i) *Spoken* or *very informal writing:* Nobody'll be out. That'll be strange. There'll probably be some accidents.	CONTRACTIONS WITH PRONOUNS AND NOUNS: *Will* is often contracted with pronouns in both speaking and informal writing: *I'll, you'll, she'll, he'll, it'll, we'll, they'll.* *Will* is also often contracted with nouns in speaking but usually not in writing, as in (h). In spoken English and very informal writing, *will* may be contracted with other kinds of pronouns and *there*, as in (i).

Be Going To

(j) Snow *is going to continue* all week. The roads *are going to* be icy. (k) *Informally spoken:* Snow's *gonna continue* all week. (l) I'm *not going to go* out. (m) *Is* the storm *going to be* dangerous?	*Be going to* also commonly expresses predictions about the future. In informal speech, *going to* is often pronounced "gonna." NEGATIVE: *be + not + going to*, as in (l) QUESTION: *be + subject + going to*, as in (m)

*Will can also be used in questions to make polite requests: *Will you open the door for me, please?* See Chart 9-8, p. 49.

3-2 Will vs. Be Going To

Prediction

(a) According to the weather report, it *will* be cloudy tomorrow.

(b) According to the weather report, it *is going to* be cloudy tomorrow.

Will and ***be going to*** mean the same when they make *predictions* about the future (*prediction* = a statement about something the speaker thinks will be true or will occur in the future).

Examples (a) and (b) have the same meaning.

Prior Plan

(c) — Why did you buy this paint?
  — *I'm going to paint* my bedroom tomorrow.

(d) — Are you busy this evening?
  — Well, I really don't have any plans. *I'll eat*/*I'm going to eat* dinner, of course. And then *I'll* probably *watch*/*I'm* probably *going to watch* TV for a little while.

(e) The meeting *will begin* at 10:00 A.M. We *will have* two hours for discussion.

Be going to is commonly used in speaking to express a *prior plan* (i.e., a plan made before the moment of speaking).

In (c): The speaker already has a plan to paint his bedroom. He could also say, "I'm planning to paint my bedroom."

NOTE: In (d), either ***will*** or ***be going to*** is possible. The second speaker has not planned her evening. She is "predicting" her evening (rather than stating any prior plans), so she may use either ***will*** or ***be going to***.

In writing, ***will*** is more common.

Willingness

(f) — The phone's ringing.
  — *I'll get* it.

(g) — How old is Aunt Agnes?
  — I don't know. She *won't tell* me.

(h) The car *won't start*. Maybe the battery is dead.

Will (but not ***be going to***) is used to express *willingness* or *offer to help.* In this case, ***will*** expresses a decision the speaker makes at the moment of speaking.

In (f): The second speaker decides to answer the phone at the immediate present moment; she/he does not have a prior plan.

Will not / ***won't*** can express *refusal,* as in (g) with a person or in (h) with an inanimate object.

Cho has a bad cough.
It ***will*** probably *be* worse by tomorrow.
She*'s **going to** go* to a doctor today.
Her husband ***will*** *drive* her there.

3-3 Expressing the Future in Time Clauses

(a) Bob will come soon. *When Bob **comes**,* we will see him.	In (a): ***When Bob comes*** is a time clause.* ***when** + subject + verb = a time clause* When the meaning of the time clause is future, the SIMPLE PRESENT tense is used. *Will* or *be going to* is not used in the time clause.
(b) Linda is going to leave soon. *Before she **leaves**,* she is going to finish her work.	

(c) I will get home at 5:30. *After I **get** home,* I will eat dinner.	A time clause begins with such words as *when, before, after, as soon as, until,* and *while* and includes a subject and a verb. The time clause can come either at the beginning of the sentence or in the second part of the sentence:
	    When he comes, we'll see him. OR
	    We'll see him *when he comes.*
	
	Notice: A comma is used when the time clause comes first in a sentence.

(d) The taxi will arrive soon. *As soon as it **arrives**,* we'll be able to leave for the airport.	
(e) They are going to come soon. I'll wait here *until they come*.	
(f) *While I **am traveling** in Europe next year,* I'm going to save money by staying in youth hostels.	Sometimes the PRESENT PROGRESSIVE is used in a time clause to express an activity that will be in progress in the future, as in (f).
(g) I will go to bed *after I **finish** my work*. (h) I will go to bed *after I **have finished** my work*.	Occasionally, the PRESENT PERFECT is used in a time clause, as in (h). Examples (g) and (h) have the same meaning. The present perfect in the time clause emphasizes the completion of one act before a second act occurs in the future.

*A *time clause* is an adverb clause. See Charts 17-1, p. 90 and 17-2, p. 91 for more information.

3-4 Using the Present Progressive and the Simple Present to Express Future Time

Present Progressive

(a) My wife has an appointment with a doctor. She *is seeing* Dr. North *next Tuesday*.	The PRESENT PROGRESSIVE may be used to *express future time when the idea of the sentence concerns a planned event or definite intention.*
(b) Sam has already made his plans. He *is leaving at noon tomorrow*.	COMPARE: A verb such as *rain* is not used in the present progressive to indicate future time because rain is not a planned event.
(c) — What are you going to do this afternoon? — *After lunch*, I *am meeting* a friend of mine. We *are going* to the mall. Would you like to come along?	A future meaning for the present progressive tense is indicated either by future time words in the sentence or by the context.

Simple Present

(d) The museum *opens* at 10:00 tomorrow morning. (e) Classes *begin* next week. (f) John's plane *arrives* at 6:05 P.M. next Monday.	The SIMPLE PRESENT can also be used to *express future time in a sentence concerning events that are on a definite schedule or timetable.* These sentences usually contain future time words. Only a few verbs are used in this way: e.g., *open, close, begin, end, start, finish, arrive, leave, come, return.*

3-5 Future Progressive

	(a) I will begin to study at seven. You will come at eight. I *will be studying* when you come.	The FUTURE PROGRESSIVE expresses an activity that *will be in progress at a time in the future.*
	(b) Don't call me at nine because I won't be home. I *am going to be studying* at the library.	The progressive form of *be going to:* **be going to + be + -ing**, as in (b)
	(c) I'*ll be picking* Susie up early for a dentist appointment. (d) We'*ll be contacting* you shortly about your inquiry.	**Will** + the progressive can be used with an activity that is not in progress at a time in the future. It is common in spoken English when the speaker wants to sound more polite or softer. It is an alternative to: 1) the non-progressive form of **will** (*I'll pick Susie up early for a dentist appointment.*) OR 2) **be going to** (*I'm going to pick Susie up early for a dentist appointment.*)

3-6 Future Perfect and Future Perfect Progressive

NOTE: These two tenses are rarely used compared to the other verb tenses.

FUTURE PERFECT	(a) I will graduate in June. I will see you in July. By the time I see you, I *will have graduated*.	The FUTURE PERFECT expresses an activity that will be *completed before another time or event in the future.* Note the sentence pattern in (a) with *by the time*: ADVERB CLAUSE *by the time* + simple present MAIN CLAUSE future perfect
FUTURE PERFECT PROGRESSIVE	(b) I will go to bed at 10:00 P.M. Ed will get home at midnight. At midnight I will be sleeping. I *will have been sleeping* for two hours by the time Ed gets home.	The FUTURE PERFECT PROGRESSIVE emphasizes the *duration of an activity* that will be *in progress before another time or event in the future.*
	(c) When Professor Jones retires next month, he *will have taught* OR *will have been teaching* for 45 years.	Sometimes the future perfect and the future perfect progressive have the same meaning, as in (c). Also, notice that the activity expressed by either of these two tenses may begin in the past.

Review of Verb Tenses

LISA: Why are there no charts in Chapter 4?
BOB: Because it's a review chapter.

CHAPTER

5

Subject-Verb Agreement

5-1 Final -s/-es: Use and Spelling

Use

(a) *Noun + -s:* *Friends* are important. *Noun + -es:* I like my *classes.*	A final **-s** or **-es** is added to a noun to make the noun plural. **Friend** and **class** = singular nouns **Friends** and **classes** = plural nouns
(b) *Verb + -s:* Mary *works* at the bank. *Verb + -es:* John *watches* birds.	A final **-s** or **-es** is added to a simple present verb when the subject is a singular noun (e.g., *Mary, my father, the machine*) or third person singular pronoun (*she, he, it*). **Mary works** = singular **She works** = singular **The students work** = plural **They work** = plural

Spelling

(c)	sing → sings song → songs		For most words (whether a verb or a noun), simply add a final **-s** to spell the word correctly.
(d)	wash → washes watch → watches class → classes buzz → buzzes box → boxes		Final **-es** is added to words that end in **-sh, -ch, -s, -z,** and **-x.** NOTE: The pronunciation is /əz/ ("uz").
(e) (f)	toy → toys buy → buys baby → babies cry → cries		For words that end in **-y:** In (e): If **-y** is preceded by a vowel, only **-s** is added. In (f): If **-y** is preceded by a consonant, the **-y** is changed to **-i** and **-es** is added.

The girl*s* and boy*s* *wear*
uniform*s* to school.

5-2 Basic Subject-Verb Agreement

Singular Verb	Plural Verb	
(a) My *friend* **lives** in Boston.	(b) My *friends* **live** in Boston.	verb + **-s/-es** = third person singular in the simple present tense *noun* + **-s/-es** = plural
	(c) My *brother and sister* **live** in Boston. (d) My *brother, sister, and cousin* **live** in Boston.	Two or more subjects connected by **and** require a plural verb.
(e) *Every* man, woman, **and** child **needs** love. (f) *Everyone* **is** here. (g) *Everybody* **is** here. (h) *Each* book and magazine **is** listed in the bibliography.		EXCEPTION: Expressions with **every** and **each** are always followed immediately by singular nouns. (See Chart 6-10, p. 32.) Even when there are two (or more) nouns connected by **and,** the verb is singular, as in (h).
(i) That *book* on political parties **is** interesting. (k) The *book* that I got from my parents **was** very interesting.	(j) The *ideas* in that book **are** interesting. (l) The *books* I bought at the bookstore **were** expensive.	Sometimes a phrase or clause separates a subject from its verb. These interrupting structures do not affect basic agreement. For example, in (i) the interrupting prepositional phrase **on political parties** does not change the fact that the verb **is** must agree with the subject **book**. In (k) and (l): The subject and verb are separated by an adjective clause. (See Chapter 13.)
(m) *Watching* old movies **is** fun.		A gerund (e.g., *watching*) used as the subject of the sentence requires a singular verb. (See Chart 14-1, p. 75.)

5-3 Collective Nouns

(a) The *audience is clapping* loudly. (b) The *team practices* at noon (c) The *faculty has chosen* a new president. (d) The *staff has been working* overtime.	Collective nouns, as in (a)–(d), refer to more than one person. In American English, singular verbs are preferred with collective nouns. NOTE: British English prefers the plural verb: *The faculty* **have** *chosen a new president.* OR *The staff* **have** *been working overtime.*
(e) The *faculty are preparing* for classes. (f) The *staff have requested* raises. (g) The *staff members have requested* raises. (h) *Members of the staff have requested* raises.	A plural verb can be used to emphasize the individual members. Note the meaning: (e) = individual faculty members (f) = individual staff members Many speakers rephrase the idea with the word *members,* as in (g) and (h), if they want to emphasize the individual members of the group.

Common collective nouns

audience	committee	faculty	group	staff
choir	crew	family	jury	team
class	crowd	government	public	

5-4 Subject-Verb Agreement: Using Expressions of Quantity

Singular Verb	Plural Verb	
(a) *Some of the **book is** good.*	(b) *Some of the **books are** good.*	With most expressions of quantity, the verb is determined by the noun (or pronoun) that follows **of**.
(c) *A lot of the **equipment is** new.*	(d) *A lot of the **printers are** new.*	For example, in (a) and (b):
(e) *Two-thirds of the **money belongs** to me.*	(f) *Two-thirds of the **coins belong** to me.*	**some of** + *singular noun = singular verb*
(g) *Twenty percent of my **income goes** for rent.*	(h) *Twenty percent of my **earnings go** for rent.*	**some of** + *plural noun = plural verb*
(i) *Most of our **homework looks** easy.*	(j) *Most of our **assignments look** easy.*	
(k) *All of the **advice was** useful.*	(l) *All of the **suggestions were** useful.*	
(m) ***One** of my friends **is** here.* (n) ***Each** of my friends **is** here.* (o) ***Every one** of my friends **is** here.*		EXCEPTIONS: ***One of, each of,*** and ***every one of*** take singular verbs. **one of** **each of** } + *plural noun = singular verb* **every one of**
(p) ***None** of the boys **is** here.*	(q) ***None** of the boys **are** here.*	***None of*** is used with a singular verb in formal English, but it is often used with a plural verb in informal spoken and written English.
(r) ***The number** of students in the class **is** fifteen.*	(s) *A **number** of **students are** late or absent today.*	COMPARE: In (r): ***The number*** is the subject. In (s): ***A number of*** is an expression of quantity meaning "a lot of." It is followed by a plural noun and a plural verb.

5-5 Subject-Verb Agreement: Using *There + Be*

(a) ***There is** a fly* in the room. (b) ***There are** three windows* in this room.	***There + be*** introduces the idea that something exists in a particular place. ***There + be** + subject + expression of place** The subject follows ***be*** when ***there*** is used. In (a): The subject is *a fly*. (singular) In (b): The subject is *three windows*. (plural)
(c) *INFORMAL:* **There's** *two sides* to every story.	In informal spoken English, some native speakers use a singular verb even when the subject is plural, as in (c). The use of this form is fairly frequent but is not generally considered to be grammatically correct.

*Sometimes the expression of place is omitted when the meaning is clear. For example, *There are seven continents.* The implied expression of place is clearly *in the world.*

5-6 Subject-Verb Agreement: Some Irregularities

Singular Verb

(a) *The United States is* big. (b) The *Philippines* **consists** of more than 7,000 islands. (c) *The United Nations has* its headquarters in New York City. (d) *Harrods is* a department store.	Sometimes a proper noun that ends in **-s** is singular. In the examples, if the noun is changed to a pronoun, the singular pronoun **it** is used (not the plural pronoun **they**) because the noun is singular. In (a): **The United States = It** (not **They**)
(e) The *news is* interesting.	**News** is a noncount noun and takes a singular verb.
(f) *Mathematics is* easy for her. *Physics is* easy for her too.	Fields of study that end in **-ics** require singular verbs.
(g) *Diabetes is* an illness.	Certain illnesses that end in **-s** are singular: *diabetes, measles, mumps, rabies, rickets, shingles.*
(h) *Eight hours* of sleep *is* enough. (i) *Ten dollars is* too much to pay. (j) *Five thousand miles is* too far to travel.	Expressions of time, money, and distance usually require a singular verb.
(k) *Two and two is* four. *Two and two* **equals** four. *Two plus two is/***equals** four. (l) *Five times five is* twenty-five.	Arithmetic expressions require singular verbs.

Plural Verb

(m) *Those people are* from Canada. (n) *The police have* been called. (o) *Cattle are* domestic animals. (p) *Fish live* under water.	*People,** *police, cattle,* and *fish* do not end in **-s**, but they are plural nouns in the example sentences and require plural verbs.

Singular Verb	Plural Verb	
(q) *English is* spoken in many countries. (s) *Chinese is* his native language.	(r) *The English* **drink** tea. (t) *The Chinese* **have** an interesting history.	In (q): **English** = language In (r): **The English** = people from England Some nouns of nationality that end in **-sh, -ese,** and **-ch** can mean either language or people, e.g., *English, Spanish, Chinese, Japanese, Vietnamese, Portuguese, French.*
	(u) *The poor* **have** many problems. (v) *The rich* **get** richer.	A few adjectives can be preceded by **the** and used as a plural noun (without final **-s**) to refer to people who have that quality. Other examples: *the young, the elderly, the living, the dead, the blind, the deaf, the disabled.*

*The word *people* has a final **-s** (*peoples*) only when it is used to refer to ethnic or national groups: *All the* **peoples** *of the world desire peace.*

Some *theories* suggest that *elephants* love their *offspring* as much as *men* and *women* love their *children*.

6-1 Regular and Irregular Plural Nouns

(a) song—*songs*	The plural of most nouns is formed by adding final **-s**.*
(b) box—*boxes*	Final **-es** is added to nouns that end in **-sh, -ch, -s, -z,** and **-x**.*
(c) baby—*babies*	The plural of words that end in a consonant + **-y** is spelled **-ies**.*
(d) man—*men* ox—*oxen* tooth—*teeth* woman—*women* foot—*feet* mouse—*mice* child—*children* goose—*geese* louse—*lice*	The nouns in (d) have irregular plural forms that do not end in **-s**.
(e) echo—*echoes* potato—*potatoes* hero—*heroes* tomato—*tomatoes*	Some nouns that end in **-o** add **-es** to form the plural.
(f) auto—*autos* photo—*photos* studio—*studios* ghetto—*ghettos* piano—*pianos* tattoo—*tattoos* kangaroo—*kangaroos* radio—*radios* video—*videos* kilo—*kilos* solo—*solos* zoo—*zoos* memo—*memos* soprano—*sopranos*	Some nouns that end in **-o** add only **-s** to form the plural. NOTE: When in doubt, use your dictionary or spell-check.
(g) memento—*mementoes/mementos* volcano—*volcanoes/volcanos* mosquito—*mosquitoes/mosquitos* zero—*zeroes/zeros* tornado—*tornadoes/tornados*	Some nouns that end in **-o** add either **-es** or **-s** to form the plural (with **-es** being the more usual plural form).
(h) calf—*calves* life—*lives* thief—*thieves* half—*halves* loaf—*loaves* wolf—*wolves* knife—*knives* self—*selves* scarf—*scarves/scarfs* leaf—*leaves* shelf—*shelves*	Some nouns that end in **-f** or **-fe** are changed to **-ves** to form the plural.
(i) belief—*beliefs* cliff—*cliffs* chief—*chiefs* roof—*roofs*	Some nouns that end in **-f** simply add **-s** to form the plural.

(j) one deer—*two deer* one series—*two series*
one fish—*two fish*** one sheep—*two sheep*
one means—*two means* one shrimp—*two shrimp****
one offspring—*two offspring* one species—*two species*
	Some nouns have the same singular and plural form: e.g.,
	  One deer is …
	  Two deer are …

(k) criterion—*criteria* (m) analysis—*analyses* phenomenon—*phenomena* basis—*bases* crisis—*crises* (l) bacterium—*bacteria* hypothesis—*hypotheses* curriculum—*curricula* parenthesis—*parentheses* datum—*data* thesis—*theses* medium—*media* memorandum—*memoranda*	Some nouns that English has borrowed from other languages have foreign plurals. In (l), the singular forms *datum* and *medium* are not commonly used. The plural forms *data* and *media* are used informally for both singular and plural.

*For information about the spelling of words ending in **-s/-es**, see Chart 5-1, p. 22.

**Fishes* is also possible but rarely used.

***Especially in British English, but also occasionally in American English, the plural of *shrimp* can be *shrimps*.

6-2 Nouns as Adjectives

(a) The soup has vegetables in it. It is *vegetable* soup.	When a noun is used as an adjective, it is in its singular form. INCORRECT: vegetable -s- soup
(b) The building has offices in it. It is an *office* building.	NOTE: Adjectives do not take a final *-s*. INCORRECT: *beautiful -s- picture*
(c) The test lasted two hours. It was a *two-hour* test.	When a noun used as a modifier is combined with a number expression, the noun is singular and a hyphen (-) is used.
(d) Her son is five years old. She has a *five-year-old* son.	INCORRECT: She has a five year -s- old son.

6-3 Possessive Nouns

Singular Noun	Possessive Form	
(a) the girl	*the girl's* coat	To express possession — the idea of belonging to someone or something, add an apostrophe (') and *-s* to a singular noun: *The girl's* coat is in the closet.
(b) Tom	*Tom's* coat	
(c) my wife	*my wife's* coat	Note in (e): If a singular noun ends in *-s,* there are two possible forms:
(d) a lady	*a lady's* coat	
(e) Thomas	*Thomas's/Thomas'* coat	1. Add an apostrophe and *-s: Thomas's* coat. 2. Add only an apostrophe: *Thomas'* coat. Pronunciation of *'s* as in *Thomas's*: /əz/

Plural Noun	Possessive Form	
(f) the girls	*the girls'* coats	Add only an apostrophe to a plural noun that ends in *-s:* *The girls'* coats are in the closet.
(g) their wives	*their wives'* coats	
(h) the ladies	*the ladies'* coats	Add an apostrophe and *-s* to plural nouns that do not end in *-s:* *The men's* coats are in the closet.
(i) the men	*the men's* coats	
(j) my children	*my children's* coats	
(k) *Alan and Lisa's* apartment is on the third floor.		Note the apostrophe usage in (k) and (l): In (k), only the final name has an apostrophe. The apartment belongs to both Alan and Lisa.
(l) *Tom's and Joe's* apartments are on the second floor.		In (l), Tom and Joe have different apartments. Both names have apostrophes.

Harry's vacation is not going very well!

6-4 More About Expressing Possession

(a) my *brother's* house (b) the *birds'* feathers (c) *Canada's* borders (d) *UNICEF's* mission	**-'s** is generally used to express possession for the following: • living creatures, as in (a)–(b); • countries, as in (c) • organizations, as in (d)
(e) the *cover of the book* (f) the *start of the race* (g) the *owner of the company*	*Of* is often used to show possession for non-living things, as in (e)–(g). NOTE: The examples in (a)–(g) show the more common usage. With some expressions, either form is acceptable: *the earth's surface* OR *the surface of the earth*. These special occurrences are best learned on a case-by-case basis.
(h) *today's* schedule (i) this *month's* pay (j) last *week's* announcement	Expressions of time do not generally take *of*. INCORRECT: schedule of today pay of this month announcement of last week
(k) people *from my country* (l) people *in my country*	When *country* is combined with *people* to show possession, the prepositions *from* or *in* are used. INCORRECT: my country's people
(m) I'll be at the *doctor's*. (n) I was at my *accountant's*. (o) I'm staying at my *cousin's*.	In (m–o), *'s* indicates a business or residence. (m) = doctor's office (n) = accountant's office (o) = cousin's home
(p) I filled out the *application* form. INCORRECT: the application's form (q) Five astronauts were aboard the *space* shuttle. INCORRECT: the space's shuttle	A noun used as an adjective can indicate *type* or *kind*, rather than possession. In (p), *application* describes the type of form. It does not express possession. In (q), *space shuttle* indicates the type of shuttle. It does not express possession.

6-5 Count and Noncount Nouns

(a) I bought *a chair*. Sam bought *three chairs*.
(b) We bought *some furniture*.
  INCORRECT: We bought some furniture ~~-s~~.
  INCORRECT: We bought ~~a~~ furniture.
			Chair is called a "count noun." This means you can count chairs: *one chair, two chairs, etc.*
			
			Furniture is called a "noncount noun." You cannot use numbers (*one, two, etc.*) with the word *furniture*.

	Singular	**Plural**	
COUNT NOUN	*a chair* *one chair*	*two chairs* *some chairs* *many chairs* *Ø chairs**	A count noun: (1) may be preceded by *a/an* or *one* in the singular. (2) takes a final *-s/-es* in the plural.
NONCOUNT NOUN	*some furniture* *a lot of furniture* *much furniture* *Ø furniture**		A noncount noun: (1) is not immediately preceded by *a/an* or *one*. (2) has no plural form, so does not add a final *-s/-es*.

*Ø = nothing (i.e., no article or other determiner)

6-6 Noncount Nouns

(a) I bought some chairs, tables, and desks. In other words, I bought some *furniture*.	Many noncount nouns refer to a "whole" that is made up of different parts. In (a): *furniture* represents a whole group of things that is made up of similar but separate items.
(b) I put some *sugar* in my *coffee*.	In (b): *sugar* and *coffee* represent whole masses made up of individual particles or elements.*
(c) I wish you *luck*.	Many noncount nouns are abstractions. In (c): *luck* is an abstract concept, an abstract "whole." It has no physical form; you can't touch it; you can't count it.
(d) *Sunshine* is warm and cheerful.	A phenomenon of nature, such as *sunshine*, is used as a noncount noun, as in (d).

(e) NONCOUNT: Ann has brown *hair*.
     COUNT: Tom has a *hair* on his jacket.
 	
(f) NONCOUNT: I opened the curtains to let in some *light*.
     COUNT: Don't forget to turn off the *light* before you go to bed.
	Many nouns can be used as either noncount or count nouns, but the meaning is different, e.g., *hair* in (e) and *light* in (f).
	
	(Dictionaries written especially for learners of English as a second language are a good source of information on count/noncount usage of nouns.)

*To express a particular quantity, some noncount nouns may be preceded by unit expressions: *a spoonful of sugar, a glass of water, a cup of coffee, a quart of milk, a loaf of bread, a grain of rice, a bowl of soup, a bag of flour, a pound of meat, a piece of furniture, a piece of paper, a piece of jewelry.*

6-7 Some Common Noncount Nouns

This list is a sample of nouns that are commonly used as noncount nouns. Many other nouns can also be used as noncount nouns.

(a) WHOLE GROUPS MADE UP OF SIMILAR ITEMS: baggage, clothing, equipment, food, fruit, furniture, garbage, hardware, jewelry, junk, luggage, machinery, mail, makeup, merchandise, money/cash/change, postage, scenery, stuff, traffic, etc.

(b) FLUIDS: water, coffee, tea, milk, oil, soup, gasoline, blood, etc.
(c) SOLIDS: ice, bread, butter, cheese, meat, gold, iron, silver, glass, paper, wood, cotton, wool, etc.
(d) GASES: steam, air, oxygen, nitrogen, smoke, smog, pollution, etc.
(e) PARTICLES: rice, chalk, corn, dirt, dust, flour, grass, hair, pepper, salt, sand, sugar, wheat, etc.

(f) ABSTRACTIONS:
—beauty, confidence, courage, education, enjoyment, fun, happiness, health, help, honesty, hospitality, importance, intelligence, justice, knowledge, laughter, luck, music, patience, peace, pride, progress, recreation, significance, sleep, truth, violence, wealth, etc.
—advice, information, news, evidence, proof, etc.
—time, space, energy, etc.
—homework, work, etc.
—grammar, slang, vocabulary, etc.
(g) LANGUAGES: Arabic, Chinese, English, Spanish, etc.
(h) FIELDS OF STUDY: chemistry, engineering, history, literature, mathematics, psychology, etc.
(i) RECREATION: baseball, soccer, tennis, chess, bridge, poker, etc.
(j) ACTIVITIES: driving, studying, swimming, traveling, walking (and other gerunds)

(k) NATURAL PHENOMENA: weather, dew, fog, hail, heat, humidity, lightning, rain, sleet, snow, thunder, wind, darkness, light, sunshine, electricity, fire, gravity, etc.

6-8 Expressions of Quantity Used with Count and Noncount Nouns

Expressions of Quantity	Used with Count Nouns	Used with Noncount Nouns	
(a) one each every	*one* apple *each* apple *every* apple	Ø* Ø Ø	An expression of quantity may precede a noun. Some expressions of quantity are used only with count nouns, as in (a) and (b).
(b) two, etc. both a couple of a few several many a number of	*two* apples *both* apples *a couple of* apples *a few* apples *several* apples *many* apples *a number of* apples	Ø Ø Ø Ø Ø Ø	
(c) a little much a great deal of	Ø Ø Ø	*a little* rice *much* rice *a great deal of* rice	Some are used only with noncount nouns, as in (c).
(d) no hardly any some/any a lot of / lots of plenty of most all	*no* apples *hardly any* apples *some/any* apples *a lot of/lots of* apples *plenty of* apples *most* apples *all* apples	*no* rice *hardly any* rice *some/any* rice *plenty of* rice *most* rice *all* rice	Some are used with both count and noncount nouns, as in (d). In spoken English, **much** and **many** are used in questions and negatives. For affirmative statements, **a lot of** is preferred. However, too + **much/many** is used in affirmative statements. *Do you have **much** time?* *I don't have **much** time.* *I have **a lot of** time.* *I have **too much** time.*

*Ø = not used. For example, **one** is not used with noncount nouns. You can say "I ate one apple" but NOT "I ate one rice."

6-9 Using *A Few* and *Few*; *A Little* and *Little*

COUNT: (a) We sang *a few* songs. NONCOUNT: (b) We listened to *a little* music.	**A few** and **few** are used with plural count nouns, as in (a). **A little** and **little** are used with noncount nouns, as in (b).
(c) She has been here only two weeks, but she has already made *a few friends*. *(Positive idea: She has made some friends.)* (d) I'm very pleased. I've been able to save *a little* money this month. *(Positive idea: I have saved some money instead of spending all of it.)*	**A few** and **a little** give a positive idea; they indicate that something exists, is present, as in (c) and (d).
(e) I feel sorry for her. She has (very) *few friends*. *(Negative idea: She does not have many friends; she has almost no friends.)* (f) I have (very) *little* money. I don't even have enough money to buy food for dinner. *(Negative idea: I do not have much money; I have almost no money.)*	**Few** and **little** (without **a**) give a negative idea; they indicate that something is largely absent, as in (e). **Very** (+ **few/little**) makes the negative stronger, the number/amount smaller, as in (f).

6-10 Singular Expressions of Quantity: *One, Each, Every*

(a) *One student* was late to class. (b) *Each student* has a schedule. (c) *Every student* has a schedule.	*One*, *each*, and *every* are followed immediately by singular count nouns (never plural nouns, never noncount nouns).
(d) *One of the students* was late to class. (e) *Each (one) of the students* has a schedule (f) *Every one of the students* has a schedule.	*One of*, *each of*, and *every one of** are followed by specific plural count nouns (never singular nouns; never noncount nouns).

*Compare:
>*Every one* (two words) is an expression of quantity (e.g., *I have read **every one** of those books*).
>*Everyone* (one word) is an indefinite pronoun. It has the same meaning as *everybody* (e.g., ***Everyone/Everybody** has a schedule*).

Note: *Each* and *every* have essentially the same meaning.
>*Each* is used when the speaker is thinking of one person/thing at a time: *Each student has a schedule. = Mary has a schedule. Hiroshi has a schedule. Carlos has a schedule. Sabrina has a schedule. Etc.*
>*Every* is used when the speaker means *all*: *Every student has a schedule. = All of the students have schedules.*

6-11 Using *Of* in Expressions of Quantity

(a) *A number of* movies came out today. (b) *A number of the* movies are available online. (c) *None of my friends* are available to watch a movie with me today.	Some expressions of quantity always include *of*: 50% of a number of three-fourths of a great deal of hundreds of a lot of thousands of a majority of millions of none of
(d) *Many* movies are available for free. (e) *Many of the* movies are free. (f) *Most of the* movies won awards. (g) *One of those* movies is really funny. (h) *Many of my* movies are in Spanish. (i) *Some of them* have subtitles.	In the following expressions, *of* is optional: one, two, etc. (of) some (of) each (of) several (of) much (of) (a) few (of) many (of) (a) little (of) most (of) hardly any (of) all (of) almost all (of) Note the difference in meaning: In (d): movies in general In (e): specific movies (e.g., online) When *of* is used with these expressions, the noun must be modified by • an article, as in (e) and (f) • a demonstrative, as in (g) • a possessive, as in (h)* Or, a pronoun can be used, as in (i). *INCORRECT:* most of movies almost movies
(j) *Every* movie had a review. (k) *No* movie is perfect.	*Every* and *no* are never used with *of*.

****All*** is an exception. Even when the noun is modified, *all* can be used without *of*: *all the movies, all those movies,* or *all my movies.*

CHAPTER 7

Articles

7-1 Articles (*A, An, The*) with Indefinite and Definite Nouns

Indefinite Nouns

(a) I had *a banana* for a snack.	An indefinite noun is a noun that has not specifically been identified.
(b) I had Ø *bananas* for a snack.	In (a): The speaker is not referring to "this banana" or "that banana" or "the banana you gave me." The speaker is simply saying that she/he ate one banana. The listener does not know or need to know which specific banana was eaten; it was simply one banana out of all bananas.
(c) I had Ø *fruit* for a snack.	
(d) I had *some bananas* for a snack.	
(e) I had *some fruit* for a snack.	Because *a** means *one*, it is not used with indefinite plural and noncount nouns, as in (b) and (c).
	Some may be used with indefinite plural count and noncount nouns, as in (d) and (e).

Definite Nouns

(f) Thank you for *the banana*.	A noun is definite when both the speaker and the listener are thinking about the same specific noun.
(g) Thank you for *the bananas*.	In (f): The speaker uses *the* because the listener knows which specific banana the speaker is talking about, i.e., that particular banana which the listener gave to the speaker.
(h) Thank you for *the fruit*.	
	Note that *the* is used with both singular and plural count nouns, as in (f) and (g), and with noncount nouns, as in (h).

Summary of Articles with Indefinite and Definite Nouns

	INDEFINITE	DEFINITE
COUNT (SINGULAR)	*a/an**	*the*
COUNT (PLURAL)	Ø, *some*	*the*
NONCOUNT	Ø, *some*	*the*

*Before vowels, use *an:* *an apple*.

7-2 Articles: Generic Nouns

A speaker uses generic nouns to make generalizations. A generic noun represents a whole class of things; it is not a specific, real, concrete thing, but rather a symbol of a whole group.

SINGULAR COUNT NOUN	In (a) and (b): The speaker is talking about any banana, all bananas, bananas in general.
(a) *A banana* is yellow.	
PLURAL COUNT NOUN	In (c): The speaker is talking about any and all fruit, fruit in general.
(b) Ø *Bananas* are yellow.	Note in (a): *A* is used with a singular count noun. No article (Ø) is used to make generalizations about plural count nouns, as in (b), and noncount nouns, as in (c).
NONCOUNT NOUN	
(c) Ø *Fruit* is good for you.	
(d) *The blue whale* is the largest mammal on earth. (e) Who invented *the wheel? The telephone? The airplane?* (f) I'd like to learn to play *the piano.* Do you play *the guitar?*	*The* is sometimes used with a *singular* generic count noun. "Generic *the*" is commonly used with: • species of animals, as in (d). • inventions, as in (e). • musical instruments, as in (f).
(g) Janice works with *the elderly.* (h) Do *the wealthy* have a responsibility to help *the poor?*	*The* is used with nouns that refer to groups of people, as in (g) and (h). Common examples include *the unemployed, the needy, the weak,* and *the sick.* These nouns are plural, and the meaning is generic. (See Chart 5-6, p. 25, for more information.)

A ride in *a hot-air balloon* is exciting.
Who invented *the* hot-air balloon?

7-3 Descriptive Information with Definite and Indefinite Nouns

(a) I'd like *a cup of coffee* **from the café** next door. (b) *The cup of coffee* **I got** was wonderful. (c) Do you have *a pen* **with red ink**? (d) *The pen* **in my bag** is leaking.	Descriptive information may or may not make a noun definite or specific. Study the examples. In (a), **from the café** *next door* does not make the *cup of coffee* definite. It is one cup of coffee among many. In (b), the speaker is referring to a specific cup of coffee — the cup that the speaker got. In (c), the speaker is referring to one of many pens, not a specific one. In (d), the speaker is referring to a specific pen.
(e) *The manager* **who trained me** got a promotion. (f) *A manager* **who trains workers** has a lot of responsibility. (g) *Managers* **who train workers** have a lot of responsibility.	Descriptive clauses may or may not make a noun specific. (e) = a specific manager (f) = any manager (g) = any managers
(h) There is *a piece of the puzzle*. (i) There is *the piece you were looking for*. (j) There are Ø *pieces on the floor*. (k) There are *the pieces you were looking for*. 	In general, *there is* and *there are* introduce new topics. Therefore, the noun that follows is usually indefinite. However, in cases where the noun is already known, **the** is used. (h) and (j) = not specific (i) and (k) = specific
(l) Jim works for *a real estate office*. (m) I stopped at *the real estate office* after work.	Adjectives do not automatically make nouns specific. (l) = one real estate office of many, not specific (m) = a specific or known real estate office

Is *a run-down house* **on a beautiful piece of property** worth *the repair headaches* **that will probably follow**?

7-4 General Guidelines for Article Usage

(a) *The sun* is bright today. Please hand this book to *the teacher*. Please open *the door*. Omar is in *the kitchen*.	GUIDELINE: Use ***the*** when you know or assume that your listener is familiar with and thinking about the same specific thing or person you are talking about.
(b) Yesterday I saw *some dogs*. *The dogs* were chasing *a cat*. *The cat* was chasing *a mouse*. *The mouse* ran into *a hole*. *The hole* was very small.	GUIDELINE: Use ***the*** for the second mention of an indefinite noun.* In (b): first mention = *some dogs, a cat, a mouse, a hole;* second mention = *the dogs, the cat, the mouse, the hole*

(c) CORRECT: *Apples* are my favorite fruit.
    INCORRECT: ~~The~~ apples are my favorite fruit.
 	
(d) CORRECT: *Gold* is a metal.
    INCORRECT: ~~The~~ gold is a metal.
	GUIDELINE: Do not use ***the*** with a plural count noun (e.g., *apples*) or a noncount noun (e.g., *gold*) when you are making a generalization.

(e) CORRECT: (1) I drove *a car*. / I drove *the car*.
      (2) I drove *that car*.
      (3) I drove *his car*.
 	
    INCORRECT: I drove car.
      I drove a that car.
      I drove a his car.
	GUIDELINE: A singular count noun (e.g., *car*) is always preceded by:
	  (1) an article (***a***/***an*** or ***the***); OR
	  (2) ***this***/***that***; OR
	  (3) a possessive adjective.

*__*The*__ is NOT used for the second mention of a generic noun. COMPARE:*
  (1) *What color is* ***a banana*** *(generic noun)?* ***A banana*** *(generic noun) is yellow.*
  (2) *Joe offered me* ***a banana*** *(indefinite noun) or* ***an apple***. *I chose* ***the banana*** *(definite noun).*

They have *a* rusty **car**, **some** broken **furniture**, and
an old **refrigerator** in ***the*** front **yard**.

7-5 Using *The* or Ø with Titles and Geographic Names

(a) We met Ø *Mr. Harper*. I go to Ø *Doctor Shue*. Ø *President Costa* is the new leader.	*The* is NOT used with titled names. INCORRECT: We met ~~the~~ Mr. Harper.
(b) They traveled to Ø *Africa*. Ø *Australia* is the smallest continent.	*The* is NOT used with the names of continents. INCORRECT: They traveled to ~~the~~ Africa.
(c) He lives in Ø *Singapore*. Ø *Canada* is a vast country.	*The* is NOT used with the names of most countries. INCORRECT: He lives in ~~the~~ Singapore.
(d) She's from *the United Arab Emirates*. *The Czech Republic* is in Europe. Have you ever visited *the Philippines*?	*The* is used in the names of only a few countries, as in (d). Others: *the Netherlands, the United States, the Dominican Republic.*
(e) He works in Ø *Tokyo*. I recently traveled to Ø *Kuwait City*.	*The* is NOT used with the names of cities. INCORRECT: He works in ~~the~~ Tokyo.
(f) *The Amazon River* is long. They crossed *the Atlantic Ocean*. *The North Sea* is in Europe.	*The* is used with the names of oceans, seas, rivers, and canals. *The* is NOT used with the names of lakes.
(g) Ø *Lake Baikal* is the deepest lake in the world. Ø *Lake Tanganyika* is the second deepest lake.	INCORRECT: ~~the~~ Lake Baikal
(h) We hiked in *the Rocky Mountains*. *The Alps* are in Europe.	*The* is used with the names of mountain ranges. *The* is NOT used with the names of individual mountains.
(i) We climbed Ø *Mount Kilimanjaro*. Ø *Mount Everest* is in *the Himalayas*.	INCORRECT: ~~the~~ Mount Everest
(j) *The Hawaiian Islands* and *the Canary Islands* are popular with tourists.	*The* is used with groups of islands. *The* is NOT used with the names of individual islands.
(k) Ari is from Ø *Tahiti*. (l) Have you ever been to Ø *Vancouver Island*?	INCORRECT: ~~the~~ Vancouver Island

Diamond Head, an extinct volcano in *the Hawaiian Islands*, overlooks *Waikiki* and *the Pacific Ocean*.

Look at those adorable triplets! I wonder if the *decision*
to wear different clothes was ***theirs***.

8-1 Pronouns and Possessive Adjectives

	Subject Pronoun	Object Pronoun	Possessive Pronoun	Possessive Adjective
SINGULAR	*I*	*me*	*mine*	*my* (name)
	you	*you*	*yours*	*your* (name)
	she, he, it	*her, him, it*	*hers, his, —*	*her, his, its* (name)
PLURAL	*we*	*us*	*ours*	*our* (names)
	you	*you*	*yours*	*your* (names)
	they	*them*	*theirs*	*their* (names)

(a) I read *a book*. *It* was good.	A PRONOUN is used in place of a noun. The noun it refers to is called the "antecedent." In (a): The pronoun *it* refers to the antecedent noun **book**. A singular pronoun is used to refer to a singular noun, as in (a). A plural pronoun is used to refer to a plural noun, as in (b).
(b) I read *some books*. *They* were good.	
(c) *I* like tea. Do *you* like it too?	Sometimes the antecedent noun is understood, not explicitly stated. In (c): *I* refers to the speaker, and **you** refers to the person the speaker is talking to. Note that the direct object cannot be omitted. *INCORRECT:* Do you like too?
(d) John has a car. **He** *drives* to work. (S above He)	SUBJECT PRONOUNS are used as subjects of sentences, as **he** in (d).
(e) Bill works in my office. I *know* **him** well. (O above him) (f) Will you talk to Bill and *me* about it? (O above me)	OBJECT PRONOUNS are used as the objects of verbs, as **him** in (e), or as the objects of prepositions, as **me** in (f). *INCORRECT:* talk to Bill and I
(g) That book is *hers.* *Yours* is over there.	POSSESSIVE PRONOUNS stand alone; they are not followed immediately by a noun, as in (g). Possessive pronouns DO NOT take apostrophes, as in (h). (See Chart 6-3, p. 28, for the use of apostrophes with possessive nouns.)
(h) *INCORRECT:* That book is ~~her's~~. ~~Your's~~ is over there.	
(i) *Her book* is here. *Your book* is over there.	POSSESSIVE ADJECTIVES are followed immediately by a noun; they do not stand alone.
(j) A bird uses *its* wings to fly. (k) *INCORRECT:* A bird uses ~~it's~~ wings to fly. (l) *It's* cold today. (m) The Harbor Inn is my favorite old hotel. *It's been* in business since 1933.	COMPARE: **Its** has NO APOSTROPHE when it is used as a possessive adjective, as in (j). **It's** has an apostrophe when it is used as a contraction of *it is*, as in (l), or *it has* when **has** is part of the present perfect tense, as in (m). NOTE: **It's** vs. **its** is a common source of error for writers of English.

8-2 Agreement with Generic Nouns and Indefinite Pronouns

(a) *A student* walked into the room. *She* was looking for the teacher.	In (a) and (b): The pronouns refer to particular individuals whose gender is known. The nouns are not generic.
(b) *A student* walked into the room. *He* was looking for the teacher.	
(c) *A student* needs to complete *his* assignments on time.	A GENERIC NOUN is not specific. It does not refer to a particular person or thing.
(d) *A student* needs to complete *his or her* assignments on time.	In (c): *A student* is a generic noun; it refers to *anyone who is a student.*
(e) *A student* needs to complete *her* assignments on time.	With a generic noun, a singular masculine possessive adjective has been used traditionally, but many English speakers now use masculine and/or feminine possessive adjectives to refer to a singular generic noun, as in (d) and (e).
(f) *Students* need to complete *their* assignments on time.	Problems with choosing masculine and/or feminine possessive adjectives can often be avoided by using a plural rather than a singular generic noun, as in (f).

Indefinite pronouns

everyone	someone	anyone	no one*
everybody	somebody	anybody	nobody
everything	something	anything	nothing

(g) *Somebody* left *his* book on the desk.	In formal English, the use of a singular possessive adjective to refer to an INDEFINITE PRONOUN is considered to be grammatically correct, as in (g) and (h).
(h) *Everyone* has *his or her* own ideas.	
(i) *INFORMAL:* *Somebody* left *their* book on the desk. *Everyone* has *their* own ideas.	In everyday, informal English (and sometimes even in more formal English), a plural possessive adjective is usually used to refer to an indefinite pronoun, as in (i).

* *No one* can also be written with a hyphen in British English: *No-one* heard me.

8-3 Personal Pronouns: Agreement with Collective Nouns

(a) My *family* is large. *It* is composed of nine members.	COLLECTIVE NOUNS can be singular or plural. When the speaker wants to refer to a single impersonal unit, a singular pronoun can be used, as in (a).
(b) My *family* is loving and supportive. *They* are always ready to help me. I love *them* very much.	When the speaker wants to refer to the individual members, a plural pronoun can be used for the pronoun, as in (b).*
(c) The *committee* meets once a month. *It* doesn't have a lot of business to take care of. OR *They* don't have a lot of business to take care of.	Choosing a singular or plural pronoun is partly a matter of judgment. In (c), both are possible.

*See Chart 5-3, p. 23, for an explanation of collective nouns.

8-4 Reflexive Pronouns

Singular	Plural
myself *yourself* *herself, himself, itself, oneself*	*ourselves* *yourselves* *themselves*
(a) Larry was in the theater. *I saw him.* I talked *to him.* (b) *I saw myself* in the mirror. *I looked at myself* for a long time. (c) INCORRECT: I saw ~~me~~ in the mirror.	Compare (a) and (b): Usually an object pronoun is used as the object of a verb or preposition, as *him* in (a). (See Chart 8-1.) A reflexive pronoun is used as the object of a verb or preposition when the subject of the sentence and the object are the same person, as in (b).* *I* and *myself* are the same person.
— Did someone email the report to Mr. Lee? — Yes. — Are you sure? (d) — Yes. *I myself* emailed the report to him. (e) — *I* emailed the report to him *myself*.	Reflexive pronouns are also used for emphasis. In (d): The speaker would say "I myself" strongly, with emphasis. The emphatic reflexive pronoun can immediately follow a noun or pronoun, as in (d), or come at the end of the clause, as in (e).
(f) Anna lives *by herself*.	The expression *by* + *a reflexive pronoun* means "alone."

*Sometimes an object pronoun is used after a preposition even when the subject and object pronoun are the same person.
Examples: *I took my books with **me**. **Bob** brought his books with **him**. **I** looked around **me**. **She** kept her son close to **her**.*

8-5 Using *You*, *One*, and *They* as Impersonal Pronouns

(a) *One* should always be polite. (b) How does *one* get to Fifth Avenue from here?	In (a) and (b): *One* means "any person, people in general." In (c) and (d): *You* means "any person, people in general."
(c) *You* should always be polite. (d) How do *you* get to Fifth Avenue from here?	*One* is much more formal than *you*. Impersonal *you*, rather than *one*, is used more frequently in everyday English. Impersonal *you* is not acceptable in academic writing.
(e) Iowa is an agricultural state. *They* grow a lot of corn there.	*They* is used as an impersonal pronoun in spoken or very informal English to mean "people in general" or "an undefined group of people." Often the antecedent is implied rather than stated. In (e): *They* = farmers in Iowa
(f) Tommy, *we* do not chew with our mouths open.	When talking to children about rules or behavior, parents often use *we*. In (f): *we* = people in general

8-6 Forms of *Other*

Singular

one   another

(a) One subject that interests me is math. *Another subject is* psychology. OR *Another is* psychology.

another = singular

Meaning in (a): one more in addition to or different from the one(s) already mentioned

ADJECTIVE FORM: **another subject** *is*

PRONOUN FORM: **another** *is*

one   the other

(b) I'm going to take two electives next term. One is sociology. *The other elective is* psychology. OR *The other is* psychology

the other = singular

Meaning in (b): all that remains of a given number; the last one

ADJECTIVE FORM: **the other elective** *is*

PRONOUN FORM: **the other** *is*

Plural

some   other(s)

(c) There are a lot of interesting movies this weekend. Some are comedies. *Other movies are* dramas. OR *Others are* dramas.

other(s) = plural

Meaning in (c): several more in addition to or different from the one(s) already mentioned

ADJECTIVE FORM: **other mov<u>ies</u>** *are*

PRONOUN FORM: **other<u>s</u>** *are*

some   the other(s)

(d) I've found several movies to watch this weekend. Some are comedies. *The other movies are* dramas. OR *The others are* dramas.

the other(s) = plural

Meaning in (d): the rest; the last ones in a group

ADJECTIVE FORM: **the other movies** *are*

PRONOUN FORM: **the other<u>s</u>** *are*

(e) I will be here for *another three years*.

(f) I need *another five dollars*.

(g) We drove *another ten miles*.

Another is used as an adjective with expressions of time, money, and distance even if these expressions contain plural nouns. *Another* means "an additional" in examples (e)–(g).

Summary of *Other/Another* Forms

	SINGULAR	PLURAL
ADJECTIVE	*another* book (is)	*other books* (are)
	the other book (is)	*the other books* (are)
PRONOUN	*another* (is)	*others* (are)
	the other (is)	*the others* (are)

8-7 Common Expressions with *Other*

(a) Mike and I write to *each other* every week. We write to *one another* every week.	***Each other*** and ***one another*** indicate a reciprocal relationship.* In (a): I write to him every week, and he writes to me every week.

(b) Please write on *every other* line.	***Every other*** can give the idea of "alternate."
	
	 The meaning in (b):
	
	     Write on the first line.
	     Do not write on the second line.
	     Write on the third line.
	     Do not write on the fourth line. (Etc.)

(c) — Have you seen Ali recently? — Yes. I saw him just *the other day*.	***The other*** is used in time expressions such as *the other day, the other morning, the other week, etc.*, to refer to the recent past. In (c): ***the other day*** means "a few days ago, not long ago."
(d) The ducklings walked in a line behind the mother duck. Then the mother duck slipped into the pond. The ducklings followed her. They slipped into the water *one after the other*. (e) They slipped into the water *one after another*.	In (d): ***one after the other*** expresses the idea that separate actions occurred very close in time. In (e): ***one after another*** has the same meaning as ***one after the other***.
(f) No one knows my secret *other than* Rosa. (g) No one knows my secret *except (for)* Rosa.	***Other than*** is usually used after a negative to mean "except," as in (f). Example (g) has the same meaning as (f).
(h) Fruit and vegetables are full of vitamins and minerals. *In other words,* they are good for you.	In (h): ***In other words*** is used to explain, usually in simpler or clearer terms, the meaning of the preceding sentence (s).

*In typical usage, *each other* and *one another* are interchangeable; there is no difference between them. Some native speakers, however, use *each other* when they are talking about only two persons or things, and *one another* when there are more than two.

CHAPTER 9

Modals, Part 1

9-1 Basic Modal Introduction

Modal auxiliaries generally express speakers' attitudes. For example, modals can express that a speaker feels something is necessary, advisable, permissible, possible, or probable; and, in addition, they can convey the strength of those attitudes. Each modal has more than one meaning or use. See Chart 10-11, pp. 56-57, for a summary of modals.

Modal auxiliaries in English

can	had better	might	ought (to)	should	would
could	may	must	shall	will	

Modal Auxiliaries

I You He She It We You They + {
can *do* it.
could *do* it.
had better *do* it.
may *do* it.
might *do* it.
must *do* it.
ought to *do* it.
shall *do* it.
should *do* it.
will *do* it.
would *do* it.
}

Modals do not take a final **-s**, even when the subject is *she, he,* or *it.*
> CORRECT: **She can** *do it.*
> INCORRECT: She ~~cans~~ do it.

Modals are followed immediately by the simple form of a verb.
> CORRECT: **She can do** *it.*
> INCORRECT: She can ~~to~~ do it. / She can ~~does~~ it. / She can ~~did~~ it.

The only exception is **ought**, which is followed by an infinitive (**to** + *the simple form of a verb*).
> CORRECT: He **ought to go** *to the meeting.*

See Appendix Chart B-1 for question forms and D-1 for negative forms with modals.

Phrasal Modals

be able to *do* it
be going to *do* it
be supposed to *do* it
have to *do* it
have got to *do* it

Phrasal modals are common expressions whose meanings are similar to those of some of the modal auxiliaries. For example: **be able to** is similar to **can**; **be going to** is similar to **will**.

An infinitive (**to** + *the simple form of a verb*) is used in these similar expressions.

9-2 Expressing Necessity: *Must, Have To, Have Got To*

Must, Have To

(a) All applicants *must take* an entrance exam. (b) All applicants *have to take* an entrance exam.	**Must** and **have to** both express necessity. The meaning is the same in (a) and (b): *It is necessary for every applicant to take an entrance exam. There is no other choice. The exam is required.*
(c) I'm looking for Sue. I *have to talk* to her about our lunch date tomorrow. I can't meet her for lunch because I *have to go* to a business meeting at 1:00. (d) Cell phones *must be* in your backpacks during class. (e) Johnny, you *must stay* away from the stove. It is very hot. (f) *Do* you *have to leave*?	In statements of necessity, **have to** is used more frequently in everyday speech and writing than **must**. The meaning in (c): *I need to do this, and I need to do that.* **Must** is typically stronger than **have to** and indicates urgency or importance. **Must** is usually found in rules, written instructions, or legal information. The meaning in (d): *This is very important!* Adults also use **must** when talking to young children about rules, as in (e). **Have to**, not **must**, is commonly used in questions, as in (f).
(g) I *have to* ("hafta") be home by eight. (h) He *has to* ("hasta") go to a meeting tonight.	NOTE: Native speakers often say "hafta" and "hasta," as in (g) and (h).

Have Got To

(i) I *have got to go* now. I have a class in ten minutes. (j) I *have to go* now. I have a class in ten minutes. (k) *Do* you *have to go* now?	**Have got to** also expresses the idea of necessity: (i) and (j) have the same meaning. **Have got to** is informal and is used primarily in spoken English. **Have to** is used in both formal and informal English. **Have to** is more common in questions, as in (k).
(l) I *have got to go* ("I've gotta go / I gotta go") now.	The usual pronunciation of **got to** is "gotta." Sometimes **have** is dropped in speech: "I gotta do it."

9-3 Lack of Necessity (*Not Have To*) and Prohibition (*Must Not*)

Lack of Necessity

(a) Tomorrow is a holiday. We *don't have to go* to class. (b) I can hear you. You *don't have to shout*.*	When used in the negative, **must** and **have to** have different meanings. Negative form: **do not have to** = *not necessary* The meaning in (a): *We don't need to go to class tomorrow because it is a holiday.*

Prohibition

(c) You *must not tell* anyone my secret. Do you promise?	**must not** = prohibition (DO NOT DO THIS!) The meaning in (c): *Do not tell anyone my secret. I forbid it. Telling anyone my secret is prohibited.*
(d) *Don't tell* anyone my secret. (e) You *can't tell* anyone my secret. (f) You*'d better not tell* anyone my secret.	**Must not** is very strong. Speakers generally express prohibition with imperatives, as in (d), or with other modals, as in (e) and (f).

*Lack of necessity may also be expressed by **need not** + *the simple form of a verb: You **needn't shout**. This is more common in British English.

9-4 Advisability/Suggestions: *Should, Ought To, Had Better, Could*

(a) You *should study* harder. You *ought to study* harder. (b) Drivers *should obey* the speed limit. Drivers *ought to obey* the speed limit.	**Should** and **ought to** both express advisability. Their meaning ranges in strength from a suggestion (*This is a good idea*) to a statement about responsibility or duty (*This is a very important thing to do*). The meaning in (a): *This is a good idea. This is my advice.* In (b): *This is an important responsibility.*
(c) I *ought to* ("otta") *study* tonight, but I think I'll watch TV instead.	Native speakers often pronounce **ought to** as "otta" in informal speech.
(d) You *shouldn't leave* your keys in the car.	Negative contraction: **shouldn't** NOTE: the /t/ is often hard to hear in relaxed, spoken English. **Ought to** is not commonly used in the negative.
(e) The gas tank is almost empty. We *had better stop* at the next gas station. (f) You *had better take* care of that cut on your hand soon, or it will get infected.	In meaning, **had better** is close to **should** and **ought to**, but **had better** is usually stronger. Often **had better** implies a warning or a threat of possible bad consequences. The meaning in (e): *If we don't stop at a gas station, there will be a bad result. We will run out of gas.* Notes on the use of **had better**: • It has a present or future meaning. • It is followed by the simple form of a verb. • It is more common in speaking than writing.
(g) You*'d better* take care of it.	Contraction: *'d better,* as in (g). In spoken English, you may not hear the "d" in **you'd**. However, "d" is necessary in writing.
(h) You*'d better not* be late.	Negative form: **had better** + **not**
(i) — I'm having trouble in math class. — You *could talk* to your teacher. OR — You *could ask* Ann to help you with your math lessons. OR — I *could try* to help you. (j) You *should talk* to your teacher. (k) *Maybe* you *should talk* to your teacher.	**Could** can also be used to make suggestions. The meaning in (i): *I have some possible suggestions for you. It is possible to do this. Or it is possible to do that.* **Should** is stronger and more definite than **could**. The meaning in (j): *I believe it is important for you to do this. This is what I recommend.* In (k), **maybe** softens the strength of the advice.*

*Two other common ways to give softer suggestions are with the expressions **might want** and **I would**: *You **might want** to talk to your teacher.* OR **I would** *talk to your teacher.* The meaning in the latter is: *If I were you, I would … .* In speaking, this is often shortened to **I would** … . You will study this verb form more in Chapter 20.

9-5 Expectation: *Be Supposed To/Should*

(a) The game *is supposed to begin* at 10:00. (b) The committee *is supposed to vote* by secret ballot.	**Be supposed to** expresses the idea that someone (*I, we, they, the teacher, lots of people, my father, etc.*) expects something to happen. **Be supposed to** often expresses expectations about scheduled events, as in (a), or correct procedures, as in (b).
(c) I *am supposed to go* to the meeting. My boss told me that he wants me to attend. (d) The children *are supposed to put away* their toys before they go to bed.	**Be supposed to** also expresses expectations about behavior. The meaning is the same in (c) and (d): *Someone else expects (requests or requires) certain behavior.* NOTE: **I am supposed to** = *I am expected to* **I suppose** = *I guess, I think, I believe*
(e) The mail *should be* here soon. (f) Amy *should be* back any minute.	**Should** can also express expectation. In (e): The speaker expects the mail to be here soon. In (f): The speaker expects Amy to be back any minute.

The management team *is supposed to discuss* plans for
the new offices tomorrow.

9-6 Ability: *Can, Know How To,* and *Be Able To*

(a) Tom is strong. He *can lift* that heavy box.	**Can** is used to express physical ability, as in (a).
(b) I *can see* Central Park from my apartment.	**Can** is frequently used with verbs of the five senses: *see, hear, feel, smell, taste,* as in (b).
(c) My husband *cannot stay* awake past 10:00.	The negative form has three options: **cannot, can't,** or **can not.** **Can not** is becoming unusual in written English.
(d) We *can't wait* any longer for Bill.	In spoken English, **can** is typically unstressed and pronounced /kən/. **Can't** is stressed and is usually pronounced /kænt/ although the "t" is often not heard.
(e) Maria *can play* the piano. She's been taking lessons for many years.	**Can** and **know how to** are used to express a learned skill.
(f) Maria *knows how to play* the piano.	In (f): **knows how to play** = **can play**
(g) I *am able to help* you now.	**Be able to** expresses ability.
(h) *Are you able to help* me I lift this?	In (g): **be able to help** = **can help**
(i) Sorry, I'*m not able to help* you. It's too heavy.	Note the question and negative forms, as in (i) and (j).
(j) Sorry, I'*m unable to help* you.	**Not able** may also be expressed as **unable,** as in (j).

9-7 Possibility: *Can, May, Might*

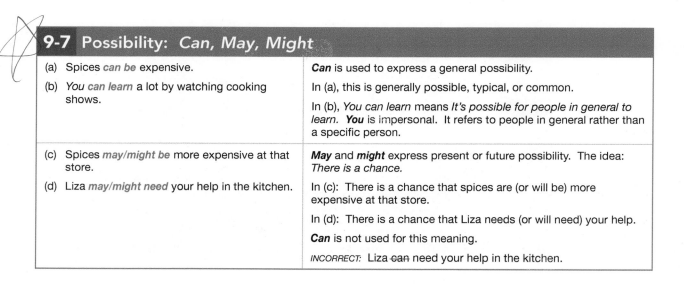

(a) Spices *can be* expensive.	**Can** is used to express a general possibility.
(b) *You can learn* a lot by watching cooking shows.	In (a), this is generally possible, typical, or common.
	In (b), *You can learn* means *It's possible for people in general to learn.* **You** is impersonal. It refers to people in general rather than a specific person.
(c) Spices *may/might be* more expensive at that store.	**May** and **might** express present or future possibility. The idea: *There is a chance.*
(d) Liza *may/might need* your help in the kitchen.	In (c): There is a chance that spices are (or will be) more expensive at that store.
	In (d): There is a chance that Liza needs (or will need) your help.
	Can is not used for this meaning.
	INCORRECT: Liza ~~can~~ need your help in the kitchen.

9-8 Requests and Responses with Modals

"I" as the Subject: *May, Could, Can*

(a) *May I borrow* your pen (please)? (b) *Could I* (please) *borrow* your pen? (c) *Can I borrow* your pen?	**May I** and **could I** are used to request permission. **May I** sounds more formal.* NOTE in (b): In a polite request, **could** has a present or future meaning, not a past meaning. **Can I** is usually considered less formal than **may I** or **could I**.
TYPICAL RESPONSES Certainly. Yes, certainly. Of course. Yes, of course. Yes, you may. Yes, you can. *INFORMAL:* Sure.	Often the response to a polite request is an action, such as a nod or shake of the head, or a simple "uh-huh," meaning "yes." Both **may** and **can** express permission. **May** is more formal than **can**.

"You" as the Subject: *Would, Could, Will, Can*

(d) *Would you pass* the salt (please)? (e) *Will you* (please) *pass* the salt?	**Would you** and **will you** in a polite request have the same meaning. **Would you** is more common and is often considered more polite. The degree of politeness, however, is often determined by the speaker's tone of voice.
(f) *Could you pass* the salt (please)?	Basically, **could you** and **would you** have the same meaning, and they are equally polite. **Would you** = *Do you want to do this please?* **Could you** = *Do you want to do this please, and is it possible for you to do this?*
(g) *Can you* (please) *pass* the salt?	**Can you** is often used informally. It usually sounds less formal than **could you** or **would you**. **May** is not possible in (g). In polite requests, **may** is only used with **I** or **we**. INCORRECT: ~~May you~~ pass the salt?
TYPICAL RESPONSES Yes, I'd (I would) be happy to / be glad to. Certainly. *INFORMAL:* Sure.	A person usually responds in the affirmative to a polite request. If a negative response is necessary, a person might begin by saying, "I'd like to, but …" (e.g., "I'd like to pass the salt, but I can't reach it.").

*__Might__ is also possible: __Might I borrow__ *your pen?* __Might I__ is quite formal and polite; it is used much less frequently than __may I__ or __could I__.

9-9 Polite Requests with *Would You Mind*

Asking Permission

(a) *Would you mind if I opened* the window? (b) *Would you mind if I used* the phone? (c) *Would you mind if I close* the door? (d) *Mind if I close* the door? TYPICAL RESPONSES No, not at all. No, of course not. No, that would be fine.	Notice in (a): **Would you mind if I** is followed by the simple past.* The meaning in (a): *May I open the window? Is it all right if I open the window? Will it cause you any trouble or discomfort if I open the window?* Sometimes, in informal spoken English, the simple present is used, as in (c). *Would you mind if I* can be shortened to *Mind if I,* as in (d). Notice that the typical response is "no." "Yes" means *Yes, I mind.* In other words: *It is a problem for me.* Another typical response might be "unh-uh," meaning "no."

Asking Someone to Do Something

(e) *Would you mind opening* the window? (f) Excuse me. *Would you mind repeating* that? TYPICAL RESPONSES No. I'd be happy to. Not at all. I'd be glad to. *INFORMAL:* No problem. / Sure. / OK.	Notice in (e): **Would you mind** is followed by the **-ing** form of a verb (a gerund). The meaning in (e): *I don't want to cause you any trouble, but would you please open the window? Would that cause you any inconvenience?* The informal responses "Sure" and "OK" are common but not logical. The speaker means *No, I wouldn't mind* but seems to be saying the opposite: *Yes, I would mind.* Native speakers understand that the response "Sure" or "OK" in this situation means that the speaker agrees to the request.

*The simple past does not refer to past time after **would you mind**; it refers to present or future time. See Chart 20-3, p. 105, for more information.

9-10 Making Suggestions: *Let's, Why Don't, Shall I / We*

(a) *Let's go* to a movie.	**let's** = **let us** **Let's** means *I have a suggestion for us.* **Let's** is followed by the simple form of a verb.
(b) *Let's not go* to a movie. *Let's stay* home instead.	Negative form: **let's** + **not** + simple verb
(c) *Why don't we go* to a movie? (d) *Why don't you come* around seven? (e) *Why don't I give* Mary a call?	**Why don't** is used primarily in spoken English to make a friendly suggestion. The meaning in (c): *Let's go to a movie.* In (d): *I suggest that you come around seven.* In (e): *Should I give Mary a call? Do you agree with my suggestion?*
(f) *Shall I open* the window? Is that OK with you? (g) *Shall we leave* at two? Is that OK?	When **shall** is used with **I** or **we** in a question, the speaker is usually making a suggestion and asking another person if she/he agrees with this suggestion, as in (f) and (g). The use of **shall** + **I/we** is relatively formal and infrequent in American English.
(h) Let's go, *shall we?* (i) Let's go, *OK?*	Sometimes **shall we?** is used as a tag question after **let's**, as in (h). More informally, **OK?** is used as a tag question, as in (i).

CHAPTER 10

Modals, Part 2

10-1 Using *Would* to Express a Repeated Action in the Past

(a) When I was a child, my father *would read* me a story at night before bedtime. (b) When I was a child, my father *used to read* me a story at night before bedtime.	*Would* can be used to express *an action that was repeated regularly in the past*. When *would* is used to express this idea, it has the same meaning as *used to* (*habitual past*). Sentences (a) and (b) have the same meaning. *Would* is more common for this purpose than *used to* in academic writing.
(c) I *used to live* in California. He *used to be* a Boy Scout. They *used to have* a Ford.	To express past situations or states, only *used to*, not *would*, is possible, as in (c). INCORRECT: *They ~~would have~~ a Ford.*

10-2 Expressing the Past: Necessity, Advisability, Expectation

PRESENT: (a) Julia *has to get* a visa. (b) Julia *has got to get* a visa. (c) Julia *must get* a visa. PAST: (d) Julia *had to get* a visa.	Past necessity: *had to* In (d): *had to* = needed to: Julia needed to get a visa. There is no other past form for *must* (when it means necessity) or *have got to*.
PRESENT: (e) I *should study* for the test. I want to pass it. (f) I *ought to study* for the test. (g) I *had better study* for the test. PAST: I failed the test. (h) I *should have studied* for it. (i) I *ought to have studied* for it. (j) I *shouldn't have gone* to the movies the night before.	Past advisability: $\left.\begin{array}{l}\textbf{\textit{should have}}\\\textbf{\textit{ought to have}}\end{array}\right\}$ + *past participle* In the past, *should* is more common than *ought to*. The past form of *had better* (*had better have*) is almost never used. The meaning in (h) and (i): *Studying was a good idea, but I didn't do it. I made a mistake.* The meaning in (j): *It was a bad idea to go to the movies. I made a mistake.* Usual pronunciation of *should have*: "should-əv" or "should-ə."
PRESENT: (k) We *are supposed to leave* now. PAST: (l) We *were supposed to leave* last week.	*was/were supposed to*: unfulfilled expectation or obligation in the past
PRESENT: (m) The mail *should be* here. PAST: (n) The mail *should have been* here by now.	*Should have* + *past participle*: past expectation The speaker expected something to happen; it may or may not have occurred, as in (n).

10-3 Expressing Past Ability

PRESENT:	(a) I *can speak* Farsi.	Past ability: ***could***
PAST:	(b) I *could speak* Farsi ten years ago.	***was/were able to***
PRESENT:	(c) I *am able to speak* Farsi.	
PAST:	(d) I *was able to speak* Farsi ten years ago.	

	(e) Maya *was able to do* well on her exam. OR Maya did well on her exam.	For a single action in the past *affirmative*, ***was/were able to*** or the simple past is used, as in (e). ***Could*** is not typically used.*
INCORRECT:	*Last week, Maya ~~could do~~ well on her exam.*	For the negative, both verbs are possible: Maya couldn't do well on the test. Maya wasn't able to do well on the test.

*Exception: ***Could*** can be used in the past for one action with these sense verbs: ***hear, feel, see, smell, taste;*** and the verbs ***understand, remember, guess.***

10-4 Degrees of Certainty: Present Time

— *Why isn't John in class?* **100% sure**: He *is* sick. **95% sure**: He *must be* sick. **50% sure or less**: {He *may be* sick. He *might be* sick. He *could be* sick. NOTE: These percentages are approximate.	*Degree of certainty* refers to how sure we are — what we think the chances are — that something is true. If we are sure something is true in the present, we don't need to use a modal. For example, if I say, "John is sick," I am sure; I am stating a fact that I am sure is true. My degree of certainty is 100%. NOTE: ***Can*** does not express degrees of certainty. INCORRECT: He ~~can be~~ sick.
— *Why isn't John in class?* (a) He *must be* sick. (Usually he is in class every day, but when I saw him last night, he wasn't feeling good. So my best guess is that he is sick today. I can't think of another possibility.)	***Must*** expresses a strong degree of certainty about a present situation, but it is still less than 100%. In (a): The speaker is saying, "Probably John is sick. I have evidence to make me believe that he is sick. That is my logical conclusion, but I do not know for certain."
— *Why isn't John in class?* (b) He *may be* sick. (c) He *might be* sick. (d) He *could be* sick. (I don't really know. He may be at home watching TV. He might be at the library. He could be out of town.)	***May, might,*** and ***could*** express a weak degree of certainty. In (b), (c), and (d): The meanings are all the same. The speaker is saying, "Perhaps, maybe, possibly John is sick. I am only making a guess. I can think of other possibilities."
(e) *Maybe* he is sick.	In (e): ***maybe*** (one word) is an adverb. In (b): ***may be*** (two words) is a verb form.

10-5 Degrees of Certainty: Present Time Negative

100% sure:	Sam *isn't* hungry.
99% sure:	{ Sam *couldn't be* hungry. Sam *can't be* hungry.
95% sure:	Sam *must not be* hungry.
50% sure or less:	{ Sam *may not be* hungry. Sam *might not be* hungry.

NOTE: These percentages are approximate.

(a) Sam doesn't want anything to eat. He *isn't* hungry. He told me his stomach is full. I heard him say that he isn't hungry. I believe him.	In (a): The speaker is sure that Sam is not hungry.
(b) Sam *couldn't/can't be* hungry. That's impossible. I just saw him eat a huge meal. He has already eaten enough to fill two grown men! Did he really say he'd like something to eat? I don't believe it.	In (b): The speaker believes that there is no possibility that Sam is hungry (but the speaker is not 100% sure). When used in the negative to show degree of certainty, *couldn't* and *can't* forcefully express the idea that the speaker believes something is impossible.
(c) Sam isn't eating his food. He *must not be* hungry. That's the only reason I can think of.	In (c): The speaker is expressing a logical conclusion, a "best guess."
(d) I don't know why Sam isn't eating his food. He *may not/might not be* hungry right now. Or maybe he doesn't feel well. Or perhaps he ate just before he got here. Who knows?	In (d): The speaker uses *may not/might not* to mention a possibility.

10-6 Degrees of Certainty: Past Time

Past Time: Affirmative

	— Why wasn't Mary in class?		In (a): The speaker is sure.
(a)	**100%:**	She *was* sick.	In (b): The speaker is making a logical conclusion, e.g., "I saw Mary yesterday and found out that she was sick. I assume that is the reason why she was absent. I can't think of any other good reason."
(b)	**95%:**	She *must have been* sick.	
(c)	**50% sure or less:**	{ She *may have been* sick. She *might have been* sick. She *could have been* sick.	
			In (c): The speaker is mentioning one possibility.

Past Time: Negative

	— Why didn't Sam eat?		
(d)	**100%:**	Sam *wasn't* hungry.	In (d): The speaker is sure.
(e)	**99%:**	{ Sam *couldn't have been* hungry. Sam *can't have been* hungry.	In (e): The speaker believes that it is impossible for Sam to have been hungry.
(f)	**95%:**	Sam *must not have been* hungry.	In (f): The speaker is making a logical conclusion.
(g)	**50% sure or less:**	{ Sam *may not have been* hungry. Sam *might not have been* hungry.	In (g): The speaker is mentioning one possibility.

10-7 Degrees of Certainty: Future Time

(a)	**100% sure:**	Kay *will do* well on the test.	→ The speaker feels sure.
(b)	**90% sure:**	Kay *should do* well on the test. Kay *ought to do* well on the test.	→ The speaker is almost sure.
(c)	**50% sure or less:**	She *may do* well on the test. She *might do* well on the test. She *could do* well on the test.	→ The speaker is guessing.

10-8 Progressive Forms of Modals

(a) Knock on the door lightly. Tom *may be sleeping*. (*right now*) (b) All of the lights in Ann's room are turned off. She *must be sleeping*. (*right now*)	Progressive form, present time: *modal* + **be** + **-ing** Meaning: *in progress right now*
(c) Sue wasn't home last night when we went to see her. She *might have been studying* at the library. (d) Joe wasn't home last night. He has a lot of exams coming up soon, and he is also working on a term paper. He *must have been studying* at the library.	Progressive form, past time: *modal* + **have been** + **-ing** Meaning: *in progress at a time in the past*

The students *may be having* fun,
but they *shouldn't be climbing* out the windows!

10-9 Combining Modals with Phrasal Modals

(a) *INCORRECT:* Janet will ~~can~~ help you tomorrow.	A modal cannot be immediately followed by another modal. In (a): The modal **will** cannot be followed by **can**, which is another modal.
(b) Janet *will be able to* help you tomorrow. (c) You *will have to* pick her up at her home.	A modal can, however, be followed by the phrasal modals **be able to** and **have to**. In (b): The modal **will** is correctly followed by the phrasal modal **be able to**.
(d) Tom *isn't going to be able to* help you tomorrow.	It is also sometimes possible for one phrasal modal to follow another phrasal modal. In (d): **be going to** is followed by **be able to**. This form is more common in negatives and questions than in the affirmative.

10-10 Expressing Preference: *Would Rather*

(a) I *would rather go* to a movie tonight *than study* grammar. (b) I'*d rather study* history *than* (*study*) biology.	**Would rather** expresses preference. In (a): Notice that the simple form of a verb follows both **would rather** and **than**. In (b): If the verb is the same, it usually is not repeated after **than**.
(c) — How much do you weigh? — I'*d rather not tell* you.	Contraction: **I would = I'd** Negative form: **would rather + not**
(d) The movie was OK, but I *would rather have gone* to the concert last night.	The past form: **would rather have** + *past participle* Usual pronunciation: "I'd rather-əv"
(e) I'*d rather be lying* on a beach in India than (*be*) *sitting* in class right now.	Progressive form: **would rather + be + ing**

Our boss *would rather not wear* a tie,
but he has to. It's company policy.

10-11 Summary Chart of Modals and Similar Expressions

Auxiliary	Uses	Present/Future	Past
may	(1) polite request (only with "I" or "we")	*May* I *borrow* your pen?	
	(2) formal permission	You *may leave* the room.	
	(3) 50% or less certainty	— *Where's John?* He *may be* at the library.	— *Where was John?* He *may have been* at the library.
might	(1) 50% or less certainty	— *Where's John?* He *might be* at the library.	— *Where was John?* He *might have been* at the library.
	(2) polite request (*rare*)	*Might* I *borrow* your pen?	
should	(1) advisability	I *should study* tonight.	I *should have studied* last night, but I didn't.
	(2) expectation	She *should do* well on the test tomorrow.	She *should have done* well on the test.
ought to	(1) advisability	I *ought to study* tonight.	I *ought to have studied* last night, but I didn't.
	(2) expectation	She *ought to do* well on the test tomorrow.	She *ought to have done* well on the test.
had better	(1) advisability with threat of bad result	You *had better be* on time, or we will leave without you.	(*past form uncommon*)
be supposed to	(1) expectation/obligation	Class *is supposed to start* at 10:00.	
	(2) unfulfilled expectation/ obligation		Class *was supposed to start* at 10:00.
must	(1) strong necessity	You *must sign* the forms in ink.	(You *had to sign* the forms in ink.)
	(2) prohibition (*negative*)	You *must not* open that door.	
	(3) 95% certainty	Mary isn't in class. She *must be* sick.	Mary *must have been* sick yesterday.
have to	(1) necessity	I *have to go* to class today.	I *had to go* to class yesterday.
	(2) lack of necessity (*negative*)	I *don't have to go* to class today.	I *didn't have to go* to class yesterday.
have got to	(1) necessity	I *have got to go* to class today.	(I *had to go* to class yesterday.)
will	(1) 100% certainty	He *will be* here at 6:00.	
	(2) willingness	— The phone's ringing. I*'ll get* it.	
	(3) polite request ˙	*Will* you please help me?	
be going to	(1) 100% certainty (*prediction*)	He *is going to be* here at 6:00.	
	(2) definite plan (*intention*)	I*'m going to paint* my bedroom.	
	(3) unfulfilled intention		I *was going to paint* my room, but I didn't have time.

Auxiliary	Uses	Present/Future	Past
can	(1) ability	I *can run* fast.	I *could run* fast when I was a child, but now I can't.
	(2) informal permission	You *can use* my car tomorrow.	
	(3) informal polite request	*Can* I *borrow* your pen?	
	(4) possibility	People *can learn* from their mistakes.	
	(5) impossibility (*negative only*)	That *can't be* true!	That *can't have been* true!
could	(1) past ability (*not for a single past event*)		I *could run* fast when I was a child.
	(2) polite request	*Could* I *borrow* your pen? *Could* you *help* me?	
	(3) suggestion (*affirmative only*)	— *I need help in math.*	You *could have talked* to your teacher.
		You *could talk* to your teacher.	
	(4) 50% or less certainty	— *Where's John?* He *could be* at home.	He *could have been* at home.
	(5) impossibility (*negative only*)	That *couldn't be* true!	That *couldn't have been* true!
be able to	(1) ability	I *am able to help* you. I *will be able to help* you.	I *was able to help* him.
would	(1) polite request	*Would* you please *help* me? *Would* you *mind* if I left early?	
	(2) preference	I *would rather go* to the park than *stay* home.	I *would rather have gone* to the park.
	(3) repeated action in the past (*not past situations or states*)		When I was a child, I *would visit* my grandparents every weekend.
	(4) polite for "want" (with "like")	I *would like* an apple, please.	
	(5) unfulfilled wish		I *would have liked* a cookie, but there were none in the house.
used to	(1) repeated action in the past		I *used to visit* my grandparents every weekend.
	(2) past situation or state		I *used to live* in Spain. Now I live in Korea.
shall	(1) polite question to make a suggestion	*Shall* I *open* the window?	
	(2) future with *I* or *we* as subject	I *shall arrive* at nine. ("will" = more common)	

NOTE: The use of modals in reported speech is discussed in Chart 12-8, p. 68. The use of modals in conditional sentences is discussed in Chart 20-3, p. 105.

The Passive

11-1 Active vs. Passive

Active: (a) <u>Mary</u> <u>*helped*</u> <u>the boy.</u> 　　　　subject　verb　object	In the passive, *the object* of an active verb becomes *the subject* of the passive verb: ***the boy*** in (a) becomes the subject of the passive verb in (b).
Passive: (b) <u>The boy</u> <u>*was helped*</u> by Mary. 　　　　　subject　　verb	Notice that the subject of an active verb follows ***by*** in a passive sentence. The noun that follows ***by*** is called the "agent." In (b): ***Mary*** is the agent. Sentences (a) and (b) have the same meaning.
Passive:　　　　　 ***be*** + *past participle* 　　　(c) He　*is*　　*helped*　by her. 　　　　　He　*was*　　*helped*　by her. 　　　　　He　*will be*　*helped*　by her.	Form of the passive: ***be*** + *past participle*
Active:　(d) An accident *happened*. Passive: (e) (none)	Only transitive verbs (verbs that can be followed by an object) are used in the passive. Here are some common intransitive verbs; they are never passive: *appear, arrive, belong, come, die, fall, happen, look like, occur, resemble, seem, sleep*. (See also Appendix Chart A-1.)

11-2 Tense Forms of the Passive

	Active			Passive			
(a) simple present	Mary	*helps*	the boy.	The boy	*is*	helped	by Mary.
(b) present progressive	Mary	*is helping*	the boy.	The boy	*is being*	helped	by Mary.
(c) present perfect*	Mary	*has helped*	the boy.	The boy	*has been*	helped	by Mary.
(d) simple past	Mary	*helped*	the boy.	The boy	*was*	helped	by Mary.
(e) past progressive	Mary	*was helping*	the boy.	The boy	*was being*	helped	by Mary.
(f) past perfect*	Mary	*had helped*	the boy.	The boy	*had been*	helped	by Mary.
(g) simple future	Mary	*will help*	the boy.	The boy	*will be*	helped	by Mary.
(h) *be going to*	Mary	*is going to help*	the boy.	The boy	*is going to be*	helped	by Mary.
(i) future perfect*	Mary	*will have helped*	the boy.	The boy	*will have been*	helped	by Mary.
(j) questions	*Is* Mary *helping* the boy?			*Is* the boy *being* helped by Mary?			
	Did Mary *help* the boy?			*Was* the boy helped by Mary?			
	Has Mary *helped* the boy?			*Has* the boy *been* helped by Mary?			
	Will Mary *help* the boy?			*Will* the boy *be* helped by Mary?			

*The progressive forms of the *present perfect, past perfect,* and *future perfect* are rarely used in the passive.

11-3 Using the Passive

(a) Rice *is grown* in India. (b) Our house *was built* in 1980. (c) This olive oil *was imported* from Crete.	Usually the passive is used without a *by*-phrase. The passive is most frequently used when it is not known or not important to know exactly who performs an action. In (a): Rice is grown in India by people, by farmers, by someone. It is not known or important to know exactly who grows rice in India. Examples (a), (b), and (c) illustrate the most common use of the passive, i.e., without the *by*-phrase.
(d) My aunt *made* this rug. (*active*)	If the speaker knows who performs an action, usually the active is used, as in (d).
(e) This rug *was made* by my aunt. That rug *was made* by my mother. (f) *Huckleberry Finn was written* by Mark Twain.	Sometimes, even when speakers know who performs an action, they choose to use the passive with the *by*-phrase in order to focus attention on the subject of a sentence. In (e): The focus of attention is on two rugs. In (f): The focus is on the book, but the *by*-phrase is included because it contains important information.

11-4 The Passive Form of Modals and Phrasal Modals

Passive form:	modal*	+	be	+	past participle	
(a) Tom	*will*		*be*		*invited*	to the picnic.
(b) The window	*can't*		*be*		*opened.*	
(c) Children	*should*		*be*		*taught*	to respect their elders.
(d)	*May I*		*be*		*excused*	from class?
(e) This book	*had better*		*be*		*returned*	to the library before Friday.
(f) This letter	*ought to*		*be*		*sent*	before June 1st.
(g) Mia	*has to*		*be*		*told*	about our change in plans.
(h) Fred	*is supposed to*		*be*		*told*	about the meeting.

Past-passive form:	modal	+	*have been*	+	past participle	
(i) The letter	*should*		*have been*		*sent*	last week.
(j) This house	*must*		*have been*		*built*	over 200 years ago.
(k) Eric	*couldn't*		*have been*		*offered*	the job.
(l) Jill	*ought to*		*have been*		*invited*	to the party.

*See Chapters 9 and 10 for a discussion of the form and use of modals and phrasal modals.

The teddy bear
will be checked first.

11-5 Stative (Non-Progresssive) Passive

(a) The door is *old*. (b) The door is *green*. (c) The door is *locked*.	In (a) and (b): **old** and **green** are adjectives. They describe the door. In (c): **locked** is a past participle. It is used as an adjective. It describes the door.
(d) I locked the door five minutes ago. (e) The door was locked by me five minutes ago. (f) Now the door *is locked*.	When the passive form is used to describe an existing situation or state, as in (c), (f), and (i), it is called the "stative" or "non-progressive" passive. In this form: • no action is taking place; the action happened earlier. • there is no *by*-phrase. • the past participle functions as an adjective.
(g) Ann broke the window yesterday. (h) The window was broken by Ann. (i) Now the window *is broken*.	
(j) I *am interested in* Chinese art. (k) He *is satisfied with* his job. (l) Ann *is married to* Alex.	Prepositions other than **by** can follow stative (non-progressive) passive verbs. (See Chart 11-6.)
(m) I don't know where I am. I *am lost*. (n) I can't find my purse. It *is gone*. (o) I *am finished with* my work. (p) I *am done with* my work.	Sentences (m)–(p) are examples of idiomatic usage of the passive form in common, everyday English. These sentences have no equivalent active sentences.

11-6 Common Stative (Non-Progressive) Passive Verbs + Prepositions

(a) I'm interested *in* Greek culture. (b) He's worried *about* losing his job.	Many stative verbs are followed by prepositions other than **by**.

be concerned be excited be worried	*about*	be composed be made be tired	*of*	be acquainted be associated be cluttered be crowded	*with*
be discriminated	*against*	be frightened be scared be terrified	*of/by*	be done be equipped be filled	
be known be prepared be qualified be remembered be well known	*for*	be accustomed be addicted be committed be connected		be finished be pleased be provided be satisfied	
be divorced be exhausted be gone be protected	*from*	be dedicated be devoted be engaged be exposed be limited	*to*	be annoyed be bored be covered	*with/by*
be dressed be interested be located	*in*	be married be opposed be related			
be disappointed be involved	*in/with*				

11-7 The Passive with Get

Get + Adjective

(a) *I'm getting hungry.* Let's eat soon. (b) I stopped working because I *got sleepy.*	*Get* may be followed by certain adjectives. *Get* gives the idea of change — the idea of becoming, beginning to be, growing to be. In (a): *I'm getting hungry* = I wasn't hungry before, but now I'm beginning to be hungry.

Common adjectives that follow *get*

angry	cold	fat	hungry	quiet	tall
anxious	comfortable	full	late	ready	thirsty
bald	dark	good	light	rich	warm
better	dizzy	hard	mad	ripe	well
big	easy	healthy	nervous	serious	wet
busy	empty	heavy	noisy	sick	worse
chilly	famous	hot	old	sleepy	

Get + Past Participle

(c) I stopped working because I *got tired.* (d) They *are getting married* next month. (e) You didn't wash the dishes. (f) The dishes *didn't get washed.*	*Get* may also be followed by a past participle. The past participle functions as an adjective; it describes the subject. The passive with *get* can be used to present information more indirectly. Note the difference in tone between (e) and (f). The passive with *get* is common in spoken English, but not in formal writing.

Common past participles with *get*

get accepted (for, into)	get dressed (in)	get invited (to)
get accustomed to	get drunk (on)	get involved (in, with)
get acquainted (with)	get elected (to)	get killed (by, with)
get arrested (for)	get engaged (to)	get lost (in)
get bored (with)	get excited (about)	get married (to)
get confused (about)	get finished (with)	get prepared (for)
get crowded (with)	get fixed (by)	get scared (of)
get divorced (from)	get hurt (by)	get sunburned
get done (with)	get interested (in)	get worried (about)

Will the student *get caught* for cheating?

11-8 -ed/-ing Adjectives

(a) — The problem confuses the students. It is *a confusing problem*.	The *present participle* can serve as an adjective with an active meaning. The noun it modifies performs an action. In (a): The noun **problem** does something; it *confuses.* Thus, it is described as a "confusing problem." The *past participle* can serve as an adjective with a passive meaning.
(b) — The students are confused by the problem. They are *confused students*.	In (b): The students are confused by something. Thus, they are described as "confused students."
(c) — The story amuses the children. It is *an amusing story*.	In (c): The noun **story** performs the action.
(d) — The children are amused by the story. They are *amused children*.	In (d): The noun **children** receives the action.
(e) It was a *delightful story*. (f) It was a *scary story*.	There are exceptions to these rules. For example, there is no adjective *-ing* form for *delight* and *scare*, as in (e) and (f).

Don was *shocked* when his son drove the family
car off the road. The much higher insurance
bill was *shocking* too.

CHAPTER 12

Noun Clauses

12-1 Introduction

(a) in the park
(b) on a rainy day
(c) her grandparents in Turkey
	Sentences contain phrases and clauses.
	A phrase
	  • is a group of words.
	  • does not contain a subject and a verb.
	  • is not a sentence.
	Examples (a), (b), and (c) are phrases.

(d) He went running in the park.
(e) She visited her grandparents in Turkey.
	A clause
	  • is a group of words.
	  • contains a subject and a verb.
	Examples (d) and (e) are clauses.

independent clause
(f) ⌐Sue lives in Tokyo.⌐
 	
independent clause
(g) ⌐Where does Sue live?⌐
	Clauses can be independent or dependent.
	An INDEPENDENT CLAUSE
	  • contains the main subject and verb.
	  • is the main clause of the sentence.
	  • may be a statement or a question.
	  • can stand alone.

dependent clause
(h) ⌐where Sue lives⌐
	A DEPENDENT CLAUSE
	  • is not a complete sentence.
	  • cannot stand alone.
	  • must be connected to a main clause.

noun clause
(i) We don't know ⌐where Sue lives.⌐
	Example (i) is a complete sentence. It has
	  • a main subject (**We**).
	  • a main verb (**know**).
	  • a dependent clause (**where Sue lives**).
	The dependent clause — where Sue lives — is also a noun clause. *It is the object of the verb **know** and functions like a noun in the sentence.*

12-2 Noun Clauses with Question Words

Question	Noun Clause	
wh + helping + **S** + **V** verb Where does she live? What did he say? When do they go?	*wh* + **S** + **V** (a) I don't know *where she lives*. (b) I couldn't hear *what he said*. (c) Do you know *when they went*?	Noun clauses can begin with question words. In (a): **where she lives** is a noun clause. It is the object of the verb **know**. In a noun clause, the subject precedes the verb. NOTE: Do not use question word order in a noun clause. Helping verbs **does, did,** and **do** are used in questions but not in noun clauses.*
S **V** Who lives there? Who is at the door?	**S** **V** (d) I don't know *who lives there*. (e) I wonder *who is at the door*.	In (d) and (e): The word order is the same in both the question and the noun clause because **who** is the subject in both.
V **S** Who are those men?	**S** **V** (f) I don't know *who those men are*.	In (f): **those men** is the subject of the question, so it is placed in front of the verb **be** in the noun clause. COMPARE: *Who is at the door?* = **who** is the subject of the question. *Who are those men?* = **those men** is the subject of the question, so **be** is plural.
What did she say? What will they do?	**S** **V** (h) *What she said* surprised me. (i) *What they will do is* obvious.	The noun clause can come at the beginning of the sentence. In (h): **What she said** is the subject of the sentence. Notice in (i): A noun clause subject takes a singular verb (e.g., **is**).

*See Appendix Chart B-2 for more information about question words and question forms.

12-3 Noun Clauses with *Whether* or *If*

Yes/No Question	Noun Clause	

Will she come?
 	
Does he need help?
	(a) I don't know *whether she will come*.
	    I don't know *if she will come*.
	(b) I wonder *whether he needs help*.
	    I wonder *if he needs help*.
		When a *yes/no* question is changed to a noun clause, **whether** or **if** is used to introduce the noun clause.
		
		NOTE: **Whether** is more common in writing and **if** is more common in speaking.

	(c) I wonder *whether or not* she will come. (d) I wonder *whether* she will come *or not*. (e) I wonder *if* she will come **or not**.	In (c), (d), and (e): Notice the patterns when **or not** is used.
	(f) *Whether she comes or not* is unimportant to me.	In (f): The noun clause can be in the subject position with **whether**.

12-4 Question Words Followed by Infinitives

(a) I don't know *what I should do*. (b) I don't know **what to do**. (c) Pam can't decide *whether she should go or stay home*. (d) Pam can't decide **whether to go or (to) stay home**. (e) Please tell me *how I can get to the bus station*. (f) Please tell me **how to get to the bus station**. (g) Jim told us *where we could find it*. (h) Jim told us **where to find it**.	Question words (**when, where, how, who, whom, whose, what, which,** and **whether**) may be followed by an infinitive. Each pair of sentences in the examples has the same meaning. Notice that the meaning expressed by the infinitive is either **should** or **can/could**.

12-5 Noun Clauses with *That*

Verb + *That*-Clause

(a) I **think** *that Bob will come*. (b) I **think** *Bob will come*.	In (a): *that Bob will come* is a noun clause. It is used as the object of the verb **think**. The word **that** is usually omitted in speaking, as in (b). It is usually included in formal writing. See the list below for verbs commonly followed by a *that*-clause.

agree that	*feel* that	*know* that	*remember* that
believe that	*find out* that	*learn* that	*say* that
decide that	*forget* that	*notice* that	*tell* someone that
discover that	*hear* that	*promise* that	*think* that
explain that	*hope* that	*read* that	*understand* that

Person + *Be* + Adjective + *That*-Clause

(c) **Jan is happy** (*that*) *Bob called*.	*That*-clauses commonly follow certain adjectives, such as *happy* in (c), when the subject refers to a person (or persons). See the list below.

I'm *afraid* that*	Al is *certain* that	We're *happy* that	Jan is *sorry* that
I'm *amazed* that	Al is *confident* that	We're *pleased* that	Jan is *sure* that
I'm *angry* that	Al is *disappointed* that	We're *proud* that	Jan is *surprised* that
I'm *aware* that	Al is *glad* that	We're *relieved* that	Jan is *worried* that

It + *Be* + Adjective + *That*-Clause

(d) **It is clear** (*that*) *Ann likes her new job*.	*That*-clauses commonly follow adjectives in sentences that begin with *it* + *be*, as in (d). See the list below.

It's *amazing* that	It's *interesting* that	It's *obvious* that	It's *true* that
It's *clear* that	It's *likely* that	It's *possible* that	It's *undeniable* that
It's *good* that	It's *lucky* that	It's *strange* that	It's *well known* that
It's *important* that	It's *nice* that	It's *surprising* that	It's *wonderful* that

That-Clause Used as a Subject

(e) *That Ann likes her new job* is clear.	It is possible but uncommon for *that*-clauses to be used as the subject of a sentence, as in (e). The word **that** is not omitted when the *that*-clause is used as a subject.
(f) *The fact* (*that*) *Ann likes her new job* is clear. (g) *It is a fact* (*that*) *Ann likes her new job*.	More often, a *that*-clause in the subject position begins with **the fact that**, as in (f), or is introduced by **it is a fact**, as in (g).

To be afraid has two possible meanings:
    (1) It can express fear: *I'm afraid of dogs. I'm afraid that his dog will bite me.*
    (2) It often expresses a meaning similar to "to be sorry": *I'm afraid you have the wrong number.*

12-6 Quoted Speech

Quoted speech refers to reproducing words exactly as they were originally spoken or written.* Quotation marks ("...") are used.**

Quoting One Sentence

(a) She said, "My brother is a student."	In (a): Use a comma after **she said**. Capitalize the first word of the quoted sentence. Put the final quotation marks outside the period at the end of the sentence.
(b) "My brother is a student," she said.	In (b): Use a comma, not a period, at the end of the quoted sentence when it precedes **she said**.
(c) "My brother," she said, "is a student."	In (c): If the quoted sentence is divided by **she said**, use a comma after the first part of the quote. Do not capitalize the first word after **she said**.

Quoting More Than One Sentence

(d) "My brother is a student. He is attending a university," she said.	In (d): Quotation marks are placed at the beginning and end of the complete quote. Notice: There are no quotation marks after **student**.
(e) "My brother is a student," she said. "He is attending a university."	In (e): Since **she said** comes between two quoted sentences, the second sentence begins with quotation marks and a capital letter.

Quoting a Question or an Exclamation

(f) She asked, "When will you be here?"	In (f): The question mark is inside the closing quotation marks since it is part of the quotation.
(g) "When will you be here?" she asked.	In (g): Since a question mark is used, no comma is used before **she asked**.
(h) She said, "Watch out!"	In (h): The exclamation point is inside the closing quotation marks.
(i) "My brother is a student," *said Anna.* "My brother," *said Anna*, "is a student."	In (i): The noun subject (**Anna**) follows **said**. A noun subject often follows the verb when the subject and verb come in the middle or at the end of a quoted sentence. NOTE: A pronoun subject almost always precedes the verb. *"My brother is a student,"* **she said**. VERY RARE: *"My brother is a student,"* **said she**.
(j) "Let's leave," *whispered* Dave. (k) "Please help me," *begged* the homeless man. (l) "Well," Jack *began*, "it's a long story."	*Say* and *ask* are the most commonly used quote verbs. Some others: *add, agree, announce, answer, beg, begin, comment, complain, confess, continue, explain, inquire, promise, remark, reply, respond, shout, suggest, whisper.*

Quoted speech is also called "direct speech." *Reported speech* (discussed in Chart 12-7) is also called "indirect speech."

**In British English, quotation marks are called "inverted commas" and can consist of either double marks (") or a single mark ('): *She said, 'My brother is a student'.*

12-7 Reported Speech

Quoted speech uses a person's exact words, and it is set off by quotation marks. *Reported speech* uses a noun clause to report what someone has said. No quotation marks are used.

NOTE: This chart presents general guidelines to follow. You may encounter variations.

Quoted Speech Reported Speech	
(a) "The world *is* round." → She **said** (that) the world *is* round.	The present tense is used when the reported sentence deals with a general truth, as in (a). ***That*** is optional; it is more common in writing than speaking.
(b) "I *work* at night." → He **says** he *works* at night. He **has said** that he *works* at night. He **will say** that he *works* at night.	When the reporting verb is simple present, present perfect, or future, the verb in the noun clause does not change.
(c) "I *work* at night." → He **said** he *worked* at night. (d) "I *am working*." → He **said** he *was working*. (e) "I *worked*." → He **said** he *worked/had worked*. (f) "I *have worked*." → He **said** he *had worked*. (g) "I *had worked*." → He **said** he *had worked*.	If the reporting verb (e.g., *said*) is simple past, the verb in the noun clause will *usually* be in a past form. Here are some general guidelines: simple present → simple past present progressive → past progressive simple past → no change or past perfect present perfect → past perfect past perfect → no change
(h) Immediate reporting: — What did the teacher just say? I didn't hear him. — He **said** he *wants* us to read Chapter 6. (i) Later reporting: — I didn't go to class yesterday. Did Mr. Jones give any assignments? — Yes. He **said** he *wanted* us to read Chapter 6.	In spoken English, if the speaker is reporting something immediately or soon after it was said, no change is made in the noun clause verb.
(j) "*Leave*." → She **told** me *to leave*.	In reported speech, an imperative sentence is changed to an infinitive. ***Tell*** is used instead of ***say*** as the reporting verb.* See Chart 14-4, p. 76, for other verbs followed by an infinitive that are used to report speech.

*NOTE: ***Tell*** is immediately followed by a (pro)noun object, but ***say*** is not: *He told **me** he was late. He said he was late.*
Also possible: *He said **to me** he was late.*

12-8 Reported Speech: Modal Verbs in Noun Clauses

(a)	"I *can* go."	→ She said she *could go.*	
(b)	"I *may* go."	→ She said she *may/might go.*	
(c)	"I *must* go."	→ She said she *had to go.*	
(d)	"I *have to* go."	→ She said she *had to go.*	
(e)	"I *will* go."	→ She said she *would go.*	
(f)	"I *am going to* go."	→ She said she *was going to go.*	

The following modal and phrasal modal verbs* change when the reporting verb is in the past:

can	→	could
may	→	may/might
must	→	had to
have to	→	had to
will	→	would
am/is/are going to	→	was/were going to

(g)	"I *should* go."	→ She said she *should go.*
(h)	"I *ought to* go."	→ She said she *ought to go.*
(i)	"I *might* go."	→ She said she *might go.*

The following modals do not change when the reporting verb is in the past:

should
ought to } (*no change*)
might

*See Chart 9-1, p. 44, for an explanation of modal and phrasal modal verbs.

12-9 The Subjunctive in Noun Clauses

(a) The teacher *demands* that we *be* on time.

(b) I *insisted* that he *pay* me the money.

(c) I *recommended* that she *not go* to the concert.

(d) *It is important* that they *be told* the truth.

Sentences with subjunctive verbs generally *stress importance or urgency.* A subjunctive verb uses the simple form of a verb. It does not have present, past, or future forms; it is neither singular nor plural. A subjunctive verb is used in *that*-clauses with the verbs and expressions listed at the bottom of this chart.

In (a): *be* is a subjunctive verb; its subject is **we.**

In (b): *pay* (not *pays*, not *paid*) is a subjunctive verb; it is in its simple form, even though its subject (**he**) is singular.

Negative: *not + simple form*, as in (c).

Passive: *simple form of* **be** *+ past participle*, as in (d).

(e) I *suggested/recommended* that she *see* a doctor.

(f) I *suggested/recommended* that she *should see* a doctor.

Should is also possible after **suggest** and **recommend.***

Common verbs and expressions followed by the subjunctive in a noun clause

advise (that)	propose (that)	it is essential (that)	it is critical (that)
ask (that)	recommend (that)	it is imperative (that)	it is necessary (that)
demand (that)	request (that)	it is important (that)	it is vital (that)
insist (that)	suggest (that)		

*The subjunctive is more common in American English than British English. In British English, **should** + *simple form* is more usual than the subjunctive: *The teacher* **insists** *that we* **should be** *on time.*

Adjective Clauses

13-1 Adjective Clause Pronouns Used as the Subject

I thanked the woman. **She** helped me. ↓ (a) I thanked the woman *who helped me*. (b) I thanked the woman *that helped me*.	In (a): *I thanked the woman* = a main clause *who helped me* = an adjective clause* An adjective clause modifies a noun. In (a): the adjective clause modifies **woman**.
The book is mine. **It** is on the table. ↓ (c) The book *that is on the table* is mine. (d) The book *which is on the table* is mine.	In (a): **who** is the subject of the adjective clause. In (b): **that** is the subject of the adjective clause. Examples (a) and (b) have the same meaning. In speaking, **who** and **that** are both commonly used as subject pronouns to describe people. **Who** is more common in writing. Examples (c) and (d) have the same meaning. In contemporary American English, **that** is preferred to **which**.** In British English, **that** and **which** are used interchangeably.
	SUMMARY: **who** = used for people **that** = used for both people and things **which** = used for things
(e) CORRECT: The book *that is on the table* is mine. (f) INCORRECT: The book is mine ~~that is on the table~~.	An adjective clause closely follows the noun it modifies.

*See Chapter 12 for information about clauses.

****Which** must be used in nonrestrictive clauses in both American and British English. See Chart 13-8.

Here are the cookies *that*
I baked for you.

13-2 Adjective Clause Pronouns Used as the Object of a Verb

The man was Mr. Jones.
I saw **him**.
↓

(a) The man	who(m)	*I saw*	was Mr. Jones.
(b) The man	that	*I saw*	was Mr. Jones.
(c) The man	Ø	*I saw*	was Mr. Jones.

Notice in the examples: The adjective clause pronouns are placed at the beginning of the clause.

In (a): **who** is usually used instead of **whom**, especially in speaking. **Whom** is generally used only in very formal English.

The movie wasn't very good.
We saw **it** last night.
↓

(d) The movie	that	*we saw last night*	wasn't very good.
(e) The movie	Ø	*we saw last night*	wasn't very good.
(f) The movie	which	*we saw last night*	wasn't very good.

In (c) and (e): An object pronoun is often omitted (**Ø**) from an adjective clause. (A subject pronoun, however, may not be omitted.)

As an object pronoun for people, **that** is more common than **who**, but **Ø** is the most common in speaking and writing.

To describe things, **that** and **Ø** are the most common in speaking. In writing, **that** is the most common, and **Ø** is rare.

SUMMARY:

    who(m) = used for people
    that = used for both people and things
    which = used for things (common in British English but not in contemporary American English)

(g) *INCORRECT:*	The man who(m) I saw ~~him~~ was Mr. Jones.	
	The man that I saw ~~him~~ was Mr. Jones.	
	The man I saw ~~him~~ was Mr. Jones.	

In (g): The pronoun **him** must be removed. It is unnecessary because *who(m), that,* or Ø functions as the object of the verb **saw**.

13-3 Adjective Clause Pronouns Used as the Object of a Preposition

She is the woman.
I told you **about her**.
↓

(a) She is the woman	about whom	*I told you.*
(b) She is the woman	who(m)	*I told you about.*
(c) She is the woman	that	*I told you about.*
(d) She is the woman	Ø	*I told you about.*

In very formal English, the preposition comes at the beginning of the adjective clause, as in (a) and (e). Usually, however, in everyday usage, the preposition comes after the subject and verb of the adjective clause, as in the other examples.

The music was good.
We listened **to it** last night.
↓

(e) The music	to which	*we listened*	*last night*	was good.
(f) The music	that	*we listened* **to**	*last night*	was good.
(g) The music	Ø	*we listened* **to**	*last night*	was good.
(h) The music	which	*we listened* **to**	*last night*	was good.

NOTE: If the preposition comes at the beginning of the adjective clause, only **whom** or **which** may be used. A preposition is never immediately followed by **that** or **who**.

INCORRECT: She is the woman ~~about who~~ I told you.

INCORRECT: The music ~~to that~~ we listened last night was good.

13-4 Using *Whose*

I know the man. **His bike** was stolen. ↓ (a) I know the man *whose bike was stolen*.	**Whose** is used to show possession. It carries the same meaning as other possessive pronouns used as adjectives: *his, her, its,* and *their*.

The student writes well.
I read **her composition**.
↓
(b) The student *whose composition I read* writes well.
	Like *his, her, its,* and *their*, **whose** is connected to a noun.
	
	    his bike → *whose bike*
	    her composition → *whose composition*
	
	Both **whose** and the noun it is connected to are placed at the beginning of the adjective clause. **Whose** cannot be omitted.

(c) I worked at a **company** *whose employees* wanted to form a union.	**Whose** usually modifies people, but it may also be used to modify things, as in (c).
(d) That's the boy *whose parents* you met. (e) That's the boy *who's* in my math class. (f) That's the boy *who's been living* with our neighbors since his mother became ill.*	**Whose** and **who's** have the same pronunciation. **Who's** can mean **who is**, as in (e), or **who has**, as in (f).

*When **has** is a helping verb in the present perfect, it is usually contracted with **who** in speaking and sometimes in informal writing, as in (f).
When **has** is a main verb, it is NOT contracted with **who**: *I know a man **who has** a cook.*

13-5 Using *Where* in Adjective Clauses

	The building is very old. He lives **there** (**in that building**).			**Where** is used in an adjective clause to modify a place (*city, country, room, house,* etc.).
(a) The building	*where*	*he lives*	is very old.	If **where** is used, as in (a), a preposition is NOT included in the adjective clause.
(b) The building The building The building The building	*in which* *which* *that* Ø	*he lives* *he lives in* *he lives in* *he lives in*	is very old. is very old. is very old. is very old.	If **where** is not used, the preposition must be included, as in (b). **In which** is more common in academic writing.

13-6 Using *When* in Adjective Clauses

	I'll never forget the day. I met you **then** (**on that day**).		**When** is used in an adjective clause to modify a noun of time (*year, day, time, century,* etc.).
(a) I'll never forget the day	*when*	*I met you.*	The use of a preposition in an adjective clause that modifies a noun of time is somewhat different from that in other adjective clauses: a preposition + **which** is used, as in (b). Otherwise, there is no preposition. The use of a preposition is very formal.
(b) I'll never forget the day	*on which*	*I met you.*	
(c) I'll never forget the day	*that*	*I met you.*	
(d) I'll never forget the day	Ø	*I met you.*	

13-7 Using Adjective Clauses to Modify Pronouns

(a) There is *someone* I want you to meet.	Adjective clauses can modify indefinite pronouns (e.g., *someone, everybody*).
(b) *Everything* he said was pure nonsense.	
(c) *Anybody* who wants to come is welcome.	Object pronouns (e.g., *who(m), that, which*) are usually omitted in the adjective clause, as in (a) and (b).
(d) Paula was *the only one* I knew at the party.	Adjective clauses can modify **the one(s)** and **those**.*
(e) Scholarships are available for *those* who need financial assistance.	
(f) *INCORRECT:* ~~I who am a student at this school~~ come from a country in Asia.	Adjective clauses are almost never used to modify personal pronouns. Native English speakers would not say or write the sentence in (f).
(g) It is *I who am responsible*.	Example (g) is possible, but very formal and uncommon.
(h) *He who laughs last* laughs best.	Example (h) is a well-known saying in which **he** is used as an indefinite pronoun (meaning "anyone" or "any person").

*An adjective clause with **which** can also be used to modify the demonstrative pronoun **that**:
   *We sometimes fear **that which** we do not understand.*
   *The bread my mother makes is much better than **that which** you can buy at a store.*

Anyone who wants to save money can come to the circus on Wednesday.
Half-price tickets are available for **those** who come on Wednesday.

13-8 Punctuating Adjective Clauses

General guidelines for the punctuation of adjective clauses:
(1) **DO NOT USE COMMAS IF** the adjective clause is necessary to identify the noun it modifies.*
(2) **USE COMMAS IF** the adjective clause simply gives additional information and is not necessary to identify the noun it modifies.**

(a) *The professor who teaches Chemistry 101* is an excellent lecturer.	In (a): No commas are used. The adjective clause is necessary to identify which professor is meant.
(b) *Professor Wilson, who teaches Chemistry 101,* is an excellent lecturer.	In (b): Commas are used. The adjective clause is not necessary to identify Professor Wilson. We already know who he is: he has a name. The adjective clause simply gives additional information.
(c) *Hawaii, which consists of eight principal islands,* is a favorite vacation spot.	GUIDELINE: Use commas, as in (b), (c), and (d), if an adjective clause modifies a proper noun. (A proper noun begins with a capital letter.)
(d) *Mrs. Smith, who is a retired teacher,* does volunteer work at the hospital.	NOTE: A comma reflects a pause in speech.
(e) *The man* { who(m) / that / Ø } *I met* teaches chemistry.	In (e): If no commas are used, any possible pronoun may be used in the adjective clause. Object pronouns may be omitted.
(f) *Mr. Lee, whom I met yesterday,* teaches chemistry.	In (f): When commas are necessary, the pronoun *that* may not be used (only *who, whom, which, whose, where,* and *when* may be used), and object pronouns cannot be omitted. INCORRECT: Mr. Lee, ~~that~~ I met yesterday, teaches chemistry.
COMPARE THE MEANING: (g) We took some children on a picnic. *The children, who wanted to play soccer,* ran to an open field as soon as we arrived at the park.	In (g): The use of commas means that *all* of the children wanted to play soccer and *all* of the children ran to an open field. The adjective clause is used only to give additional information about the children.
(h) We took some children on a picnic. *The children who wanted to play soccer* ran to an open field as soon as we arrived at the park. The others played a different game.	In (h): The lack of commas means that *only some* of the children wanted to play soccer. The adjective clause is used to identify which children ran to the open field.

*Adjective clauses that do not require commas are called *essential* or *restrictive* or *identifying*.
**Adjective clauses that require commas are called *nonessential* or *nonrestrictive* or *nonidentifying*.
NOTE: Nonessential adjective clauses are more common in writing than in speaking.

13-9 Using Expressions of Quantity in Adjective Clauses

In my class there are 20 students. *Most of them* are from Asia. (a) In my class there are 20 students, *most of whom* are from Asia.	An adjective clause may contain an expression of quantity with *of: some of, many of, most of, none of, two of, half of, both of,* etc.
(b) He gave several reasons, *only a few of which* were valid.	The expression of quantity precedes the pronoun. Only *whom, which,* and *whose* are used in this pattern.
(c) The teachers discussed Jim, *one of whose problems* was poor study habits.	This pattern is more common in writing than speaking. Commas are used.

13-10 Using *Which* to Modify a Whole Sentence

(a) Tom was late. ***That*** surprised me. (b) Tom was late, *which surprised me*. (c) The elevator is out of order. ***This*** is too bad. (d) The elevator is out of order, *which is too bad*.	The pronouns ***that*** and ***this*** can refer to the idea of a whole sentence which comes before. In (a): The word ***that*** refers to the whole sentence ***Tom was late***. Similarly, an adjective clause with ***which*** may modify the idea of a whole sentence. In (b): The word ***which*** refers to the whole sentence ***Tom was late***. Using ***which*** to modify a whole sentence is informal and occurs most frequently in spoken English. This structure is generally not appropriate in formal writing. Whenever it is written, however, it is preceded by a comma to reflect a pause in speech.

13-11 Reducing Adjective Clauses to Adjective Phrases

CLAUSE: *A clause is a group of related words that contains a subject and a verb.*
PHRASE: *A phrase is a group of related words that does not contain a subject and a verb.*

(a) CLAUSE: The girl *who is sitting next to me* is Mai. (b) PHRASE: The girl *sitting next to me* is Mai. (c) CLAUSE: The girl *(whom) I saw* was Mai. (d) PHRASE: *(none)*	An adjective phrase is a reduction of an adjective clause. It modifies a noun. It does not contain a subject and verb. Examples (a) and (b) have the same meaning. Only adjective clauses that have a subject pronoun — ***who***, ***that***, or ***which*** — can be reduced to modifying adjective phrases. The adjective clause in (c) cannot be reduced to an adjective phrase.

(e) CLAUSE: The man *who is talking* to John is from Korea.
    PHRASE: The man Ø Ø *talking* to John is from Korea.
 	
(f) CLAUSE: The ideas *that are presented* in this book are good.
    PHRASE: The ideas Ø Ø *presented* in this book are good.
 	
(g) CLAUSE: Ann is the woman *that is responsible* for the error.
    PHRASE: Ann is the woman Ø Ø *responsible* for the error.
	There are two ways in which an adjective clause is changed to an adjective phrase.
	
	1. if the adjective clause contains the ***be*** form of a verb, omit the subject pronoun and the ***be*** form, as in (e), (f), and (g).*

(h) CLAUSE: English has an alphabet *that consists* of 26 letters.
    PHRASE: English has an alphabet Ø *consisting* of 26 letters.
 	
(i) CLAUSE: Anyone *who wants*   to come with us is welcome.
    PHRASE: Anyone Ø *wanting* to come with us is welcome.
	2. If there is no ***be*** form of a verb in the adjective clause, it is sometimes possible to omit the subject pronoun and change the verb to its ***-ing*** form, as in (h) and (i).

(j) ***Paris***, *which is the capital of France*, is an exciting city. (k) ***Paris***, *the capital of France*, is an exciting city.	If the adjective clause requires commas, as in (j), the adjective phrase also requires commas, as in (k). An adjective phrase in which a noun follows another noun, as in (k), is called an *appositive*.

*If an adjective clause that contains ***be*** + *a single adjective* is changed, the adjective is moved to its normal position in front of the noun it modifies.

> CLAUSE: ***Fruit that is fresh*** *tastes better than old, soft, mushy fruit.*
> CORRECT PHRASE: ***Fresh fruit*** *tastes better than old, soft, mushy fruit.*
> *INCORRECT PHRASE:* *Fruit fresh tastes better than old, soft, mushy fruit.*

CHAPTER 14

Gerunds and Infinitives, Part 1

14-1 Gerunds and Infinitives: Introduction

(a) **S** *Playing* tennis **V** *is* fun.	A *gerund* is the **-ing** form of a verb used as a noun. A gerund is used in the same ways as a noun, i.e., as a subject or as an object.
(b) **S** We **V** enjoy **O** *playing* tennis.	In (a): *playing* is a gerund. It is used as the subject of the sentence. **Playing tennis** is a *gerund phrase*.
(c) He's excited **PREP** about **O** *playing* tennis.	In (b): *playing* is a gerund used as the object of the verb *enjoy*. In (c): *playing* is a gerund used as the object of the preposition *about*.
(d) **S** *To play* tennis well **V** *takes* a lot of practice.	An *infinitive* = **to** + *the simple form of a verb* (*to see, to be, to go*, etc.).
(e) **S** He **V** likes **O** *to play* tennis.	Like gerunds, infinitives can also be used as the subject of a sentence, as in (d), or as the object, as in (e), but it is more common for the infinitive to be used as the object.

14-2 Common Verbs Followed by Gerunds

(a) I verb *enjoy* + gerund *playing* tennis.	Gerunds can be used as the objects of certain verbs. In (a): *enjoy* is followed by a gerund (*playing*). *Enjoy* is not followed by an infinitive. *INCORRECT*: I enjoy ~~to play~~ tennis. Common verbs that are followed by gerunds are listed below.
(b) Joe *quit smoking*. (c) Joe *gave up smoking*.	Some phrasal verbs are followed by gerunds. A *phrasal verb* consists of a verb and a particle (a small word such as a preposition) that together have a special meaning. For example in (c), *give up* means "quit." (Phrasal verbs are in parentheses below.)

Verb + gerund

enjoy	quit (give up)	avoid	consider
appreciate	finish (get through)	postpone (put off)	discuss
mind	stop*	delay	mention
		keep (keep on)	suggest**

*Stop can also be followed by an infinitive of purpose. *He **stopped** at the station (**in order**) to get some gas.* See
Charts 14-5 and 15-1, p. 83.

**Suggest can also be used with a subjunctive noun clause. See Chart 12-9. p. 68.

14-3 Common Verbs Followed by Infinitives

(a) I *hope to see* you again soon.	Some verbs are followed immediately by an infinitive, as in (a) and (b).
(b) He *promised to be* here by ten.	
(c) He *promised not to be* late.	Negative form: ***not*** precedes the infinitive, as in (c).

Common verbs followed by infinitives

hope to (do something)	promise to	seem to	expect to
plan to	agree to	appear to	would like to
intend to*	offer to	pretend to	want to
decide to	refuse to	ask to	need to

*****Intend** is usually followed by an infinitive (*I **intend to go** to the meeting.*) but sometimes may be followed by a gerund (*I **intend going** to the meeting.*) with no change in meaning.

14-4 Infinitives with Objects

Verb + Object + Infinitive

(a) Mr. Lee *told me to be* here at ten o'clock.	Some verbs are followed by a pronoun or noun object and then an infinitive, as in (a) and (b).
(b) The police *ordered the driver to stop*.	
(c) I *was told to be* here at ten o'clock.	These verbs are followed immediately by an infinitive when they are used in the passive, as in (c) and (d).
(d) The driver *was ordered* to stop.	

Common verbs followed by noun or pronoun + infinitive

tell someone to	invite someone to	require someone to	expect someone to
advise someone to*	permit someone to	order someone to	would like someone to
encourage someone to	allow someone to	force someone to	want someone to
remind someone to	warn someone to	ask someone to	need someone to

Verb + Infinitive / Verb + Object + Infinitive

(e) I *expect to pass* the test.	Some verbs have two patterns:
(f) I *expect Mary to pass* the test.	• *verb + infinitive*, as in (e) • *verb + object + infinitive*, as in (f)
	COMPARE: In (e): I think I will pass the test. In (f): I think Mary will pass the test.

Common verbs followed by infinitives or by objects and then infinitives

ask to OR ask someone to	want to OR want someone to
expect to OR expect someone to	would like to OR would like someone to
need to OR need someone to	

*A gerund is used after ***advise*** (active) if there is no noun or pronoun object.
COMPARE: (1) *He advised buying a Fiat.* (2) *He advised me to buy a Fiat. I was advised to buy a Fiat.*

14-5 Common Verbs Followed by Either Infinitives or Gerunds

Some verbs can be followed by either an infinitive or a gerund, sometimes with no difference in meaning, as in Group A below, and sometimes with a difference in meaning, as in Group B below.

Group A: Verb + Infinitive or Gerund, with No Difference in Meaning

begin start continue	like love prefer	hate can't stand can't bear	The verbs in Group A may be followed by either an infinitive or a gerund with little or no difference in meaning.
(a) It *began to rain*. / It *began raining*. (b) I *started to work*. / I *started working*.			In (a): There is no difference between ***began to rain*** and ***began raining***.
(c) It *was beginning to rain*.			If the main verb is progressive, an infinitive (not a gerund) is usually used, as in (c).

Group B: Verb + Infinitive or Gerund, with a Difference in Meaning

remember forget	regret try	stop	The verbs in Group B may be followed by either an infinitive or a gerund, but the meaning is different.
(d) Judy always *remembers to lock* the door.			***remember*** + *infinitive* = remember to perform responsibility, duty, or task, as in (d)
(e) Sam often *forgets to lock* the door.			***forget*** + *infinitive* = forget to perform a responsibility, duty, or task, as in (e)
(f) I *remember seeing* the Alps for the first time. The sight was impressive.			***remember*** + *gerund* = remember (recall) something that happened in the past, as in (f)
(g) I'*ll never forget seeing* the Alps for the first time.			***forget*** + *gerund* = forget something that happened in the past, as in (g)*
(h) I *regret to tell* you that you failed the test.			***regret*** + *infinitive* = regret to say, to tell someone, to inform someone of some bad news, as in (h)
(i) I *regret lending* him some money. He never paid me back.			***regret*** + *gerund* = regret something that happened in the past, as in (i)
(j) I'*m trying to learn* English.			***try*** + *infinitive* = make an effort, as in (j)
(k) The room was hot. I *tried opening* the window, but that didn't help. So I *tried turning* on the fan, but I was still hot. Finally, I turned on the air conditioner.			***try*** + *gerund* = experiment with a new or different approach to see if it works, as in (k)
(l) The students *stopped talking* when the professor entered the room. The room became quiet.			***stop*** + *gerund* = stop an activity
(m) When Ann saw her professor in the hallway, she *stopped (in order) to talk* to him.			Notice that ***stop*** can also be followed immediately by an infinitive of purpose, as in (m): Ann stopped walking in order to talk to her professor. (See Chart 15-1, p. 83.)

*__Forget__ followed by a gerund usually occurs in a negative sentence or in a question: e.g., *I'll never forget, I can't forget, Have you ever forgotten,* and *Can you ever forget* are often followed by a gerund phrase.

Why is the safe open?
Did you **forget to lock** it?

14-6 Using Gerunds as the Objects of Prepositions

(a) We talked *about going* to Iceland for our vacation. (b) Sue is in charge *of organizing* the meeting. (c) I'm interested *in learning* more about your work.	A gerund is frequently used as the object of a preposition.
(d) *I'm used to sleeping* with the window open. (e) *I'm accustomed to sleeping** with the window open. (f) I *look forward to going* home next month.	In (d) through (f): **to** is a preposition, not part of an infinitive form, so a gerund follows.
(g) We *talked about not going* to the meeting, but finally decided we should go.	NEGATIVE FORM: **not** precedes a gerund.

Common preposition combinations followed by gerunds

be excited** } *about doing it*
be worried }

complain }
dream }
talk } *about /of doing it*
think }
apologize }

blame someone }
forgive someone }
have an excuse }
have a reason } *for doing it*
be responsible }
thank someone }

keep someone }
prevent someone }
prohibit someone } *from doing it*
stop someone }

be interested }
believe }
participate } *in doing it*
succeed }

approve }
be accused }
be afraid** }
be capable }
be guilty } *of doing it*
be proud** }
instead }
take advantage }
take care }

be tired } *of /from doing it*

count } *on doing* it
insist }

be accustomed }
in addition }
be committed }
be devoted }
look forward } *to doing it*
object }
be opposed }
be used }

*Possible in British English: *I'm accustomed to sleep with the window open.*
**Be afraid, be excited,* and *be proud* can also be used with an infinitive. See Chart 15-2, page 83.

14-7 Go + Gerund

(a) Did you *go shopping*? (b) We *went fishing* yesterday.	**Go** is followed by a gerund in certain idiomatic expressions to express, for the most part, recreational activities.

Go + gerund

go biking	go dancing	go running	go skiing
go birdwatching	go fishing*	go sailing	go skydiving
go boating	go hiking	go shopping	go sledding
go bowling	go hunting	go sightseeing	go snorkeling
go camping	go jogging	go skating	go swimming
go canoeing / kayaking	go mountain climbing	go skateboarding	go window shopping

*Also, in British English: *go angling.*

14-8 Special Expressions Followed by -ing

(a) We *had fun* We *had a good time* } *playing* volleyball. (b) I *had trouble* I *had difficulty* I *had a hard time* I *had a difficult time* } *finding* his house.	*-ing* forms follow certain special expressions: **have fun / a good time** + **-ing** **have trouble / difficulty** + **-ing** **have a hard time / a difficult time** + **-ing**
(c) Sam *spends* most of his time *studying*. (d) I *waste* a lot of time *watching* TV.	**spend** + *expression of time or money* + **-ing** **waste** + *expression of time or money* + **-ing**
(e) She *sat* at her desk *doing* homework. (f) I *stood* there *wondering* what to do next. (g) He *is lying* in bed *reading* a book.	**sit** + *expression of place* + **-ing** **stand** + *expression of place* + **-ing** **lie** + *expression of place* + **-ing**
(h) When I walked into my office, I *found George using* my telephone. (i) When I walked into my office, I *caught* a thief *looking* through my desk drawers.	**find** + *(pro)noun* + **-ing** **catch** + *(pro)noun* + **-ing** In (h) and (i): Both **find** and **catch** mean "discover." **Catch** often expresses anger or displeasure.

14-9 *It* + Infinitive; Gerunds and Infinitives as Subjects

(a) *It* is difficult *to learn* a second language.	Often an infinitive phrase is used with *it* as the subject of a sentence. The word *it* refers to and has the same meaning as the infinitive phrase at the end of the sentence. In (a): *It* means "to learn a second language."
(b) *Learning* a second language is difficult.	A gerund phrase is frequently used as the subject of a sentence, as in (b).
(c) *To learn* a second language is difficult.	An infinitive can also be used as the subject of a sentence, as in (c), but far more commonly an infinitive phrase is used with *it*, as in (a).
(d) It is easy *for young children* to learn a second language. *Learning a second language* is easy *for young children*. *To learn a second language* is easy *for young children*.	The phrase **for (someone)** may be used to specify exactly who the speaker is talking about, as in (d).

14-10 Reference List of Verbs Followed by Infinitives

Verbs with a bullet (•) can also be followed by gerunds. See Chart 14-11.

Verbs Followed Immediately by an Infinitive

1.	agree	They *agreed to help* us.
2.	appear	She *appears to be* tired.
3.	arrange	I'll *arrange to meet* you at the airport.
4.	ask	He *asked to come* with us.
5.	beg	He *begged to come* with us.
6.	begin•	It *began to rain*.
7.	can't afford	I *can't afford to buy* it.
8.	can't bear•	I *can't bear to wait* in long lines.
9.	can't stand•	I *can't stand to wait* in long lines.
10.	can't wait	We *can't wait to see* you.
11.	care	I *don't care to see* that show.
12.	claim	She *claims to know* a famous movie star.
13.	consent	She finally *consented to marry* him.
14.	continue•	He *continued to speak*.
15.	decide	I have *decided to leave* on Monday.
16.	demand	I *demand to know* who is responsible.
17.	deserve	She *deserves to win* the prize.
18.	expect	I *expect to enter* graduate school in the fall.
19.	fail	She *failed to return* the book to the library on time.
20.	forget•	I *forgot to mail* the letter.
21.	hate•	I *hate to make* silly mistakes.
22.	hesitate	Don't *hesitate to ask* for my help.
23.	hope	Jack *hopes to arrive* next week.
24.	intend	He *intends to be* a firefighter.
25.	learn	He *learned to play* the piano.
26.	like•	I *like to go* to the movies.
27.	love•	I *love to go* to operas.
28.	manage	She *managed to finish* her work early.
29.	mean	I didn't *mean to hurt* your feelings.
30.	need	I *need to have* your opinion.
31.	offer	They *offered to help* us.
32.	plan	I'm *planning to have* a party.
33.	prefer•	Ann *prefers to walk* to work.
34.	prepare	We *prepared to welcome* them.
35.	pretend	He *pretends not to understand*.
36.	promise	I *promise not to be* late.
37.	refuse	I *refuse to believe* his story.
38.	regret•	I *regret to tell* you that you failed.
39.	remember•	I *remembered to lock* the door.
40.	seem	That cat *seems to be* friendly.
41.	start•	It *started to rain*.
42.	stop	Let's *stop to get* a snack.
43.	struggle	I *struggled to stay* awake.
44.	swear	She *swore to tell* the truth.
45.	tend	He *tends to talk* too much.
46.	threaten	She *threatened to tell* my parents.
47.	try•	I'm *trying to learn* English.
48.	volunteer	He *volunteered to help* us.
49.	wait	I'll *wait to hear* from you.
50.	want	I *want to tell* you something.
51.	wish	She *wishes to come* with us.

Verbs Followed by a (Pro)noun + an Infinitive

1.	advise•	She *advised me to wait* until tomorrow.
2.	allow	She *allowed me to use* her car.
3.	ask	I *asked John to help* us.
4.	beg	They *begged us to come*.
5.	cause	Her laziness *caused her to fail*.
6.	challenge	She *challenged me to race* her to the corner.
7.	convince	I couldn't *convince him to accept* our help.
8.	dare	He *dared me to do* better than he had done.
9.	encourage	He *encouraged me to try* again.
10.	expect	I *expect you to be* on time.
11.	forbid	I *forbid you to tell* him.
12.	force	They *forced him to tell* the truth.
13.	hire	She *hired a boy to mow* the lawn.
14.	instruct	He *instructed them to be* careful.
15.	invite	Harry *invited the Johnsons to come* to his party.
16.	need	We *needed Chris to help* us figure out the solution.
17.	order	The judge *ordered me to pay* a fine.
18.	permit	He *permitted the children to stay* up late.
19.	persuade	I *persuaded him to come* for a visit.
20.	remind	She *reminded me to lock* the door.
21.	require	Our teacher *requires us to be* on time.
22.	teach	My brother *taught me to swim*.
23.	tell	The doctor *told me to take* these pills.
24.	urge	I *urged her to apply* for the job.
25.	want	I *want you to be* happy.
26.	warn	I *warned you not to drive* too fast.

14-11 Reference List of Verbs Followed by Gerunds

Verbs with a bullet (•) can also be followed by infinitives. See Chart 14-10.

1.	admit	He *admitted stealing* the money.
2.	advise•	She *advised waiting* until tomorrow.
3.	anticipate	I *anticipate having* a good time on vacation.
4.	appreciate	I *appreciated hearing* from them.
5.	avoid	He *avoided answering* my question.
6.	begin•	It *began raining*.
7.	can't bear•	I *can't bear waiting* in long lines.
8.	can't help	I *can't help worrying* about it.
9.	can't imagine	I can't *imagine having* no friends.
10.	can't stand•	I *can't stand waiting* in long lines.
11.	complete	I finally *completed writing* my term paper.
12.	consider	I *will consider going* with you.
13.	continue•	He *continued speaking*.
14.	delay	He *delayed leaving* for school.
15.	deny	She *denied committing* the crime.
16.	discuss	They *discussed opening* a new business.
17.	dislike	I *dislike driving* long distances.
18.	enjoy	We *enjoyed visiting* them.
19.	finish	She *finished studying* about ten.
20.	forget•	I'll *never forget visiting* Napoleon's tomb.
21.	hate•	I *hate making* silly mistakes.
22.	imagine	I *imagined* getting a scholarship, and I did.
23.	keep	I *keep hoping* he will come.
24.	like•	I *like going* to movies.
25.	love•	I *love going* to operas.
26.	mention	She *mentioned going* to a movie.
27.	mind	*Would* you *mind helping* me with this?
28.	miss	I *miss being* with my family.
29.	postpone	Let's *postpone leaving* until tomorrow.
30.	practice	The athlete *practiced throwing* the ball.
31.	prefer•	Ann *prefers walking* to driving to work.
32.	quit	He *quit trying* to solve the problem.
33.	recall	I *don't recall meeting* him before.
34.	recollect	I *don't recollect meeting* him before.
35.	recommend	She *recommended seeing* the show.
36.	regret•	I *regret telling* him my secret.
37.	remember•	I *can remember meeting* him when I was a child.
38.	resent	I *resent her interfering* in my business.
39.	resist	I *couldn't resist eating* the dessert.
40.	risk	She *risks losing* all of her money.
41.	start•	It *started raining*.
42.	stop	She *stopped going* to classes when she got sick.
43.	suggest	She *suggested going* to a movie.
44.	tolerate	She *won't tolerate cheating* during an examination.
45.	try•	I *tried changing* the light bulb, but the lamp still didn't work.
46.	understand	I *don't understand his leaving* school.
47.	urge	The official *urged using* caution.

14-12 Reference List of Preposition Combinations Followed by Gerunds

Preposition Combinations + Gerunds

1. apologize for	He *apologized for forgetting* his wife's birthday.	14. look forward to	I'm *looking forward to going* home.
2. approve of	The company manager *approved of hiring* me.	15. object to	The voters *objected to increasing* taxes.
3. blame someone for	She *blamed him for stealing* her phone.	16. participate in	The entire staff *participated in welcoming* students on the first day.
4. complain about / of	She *complained about working* too hard.	17. prevent someone from	Will the medicine *prevent me from getting* sick?
5. count on	I'm *counting on going* with you.	18. prohibit someone from	The police *prohibited them from leaving*.
6. dream about / of	He *dreamed about / of flying* an airplane	19. stop someone from	Security *stopped a passenger from getting* on the subway.
7. forgive someone for	She *forgave him for lying*.	20. succeed in	He *succeeded in getting* the job.
8. have a reason for	He *had a reason for being* absent.	21. take advantage of	I'm *taking advantage of having* a free day tomorrow.
9. have an excuse for	Did you *have an excuse for leaving* early?	22. take care of	She *took care of filling* out the paperwork.
10. in addition to	*In addition to studying*, I have to work this weekend.	23. talk about / of	He talked *about / of feeling* homesick.
11. insist on	I *insist on coming* with you.	24. thank someone for	They *thanked him for coming*.
12. instead of	*Instead of sitting* there, why don't you help us?	25. think about / of	She *thought about quitting* her job.
13. keep someone from	Can a special pillow *keep you from snoring*?		

Preposition Combinations with *Be* + Gerunds

1. be accused of	He *was accused of stealing*.	9. be interested in	I *am interested in learning* more about your country.
2. be accustomed to	She *is accustomed to working* hard.	10. be opposed to	He *is opposed to going* to war.
3. be afraid of	My kids *are afraid of being* alone.	11. be proud of	She *was proud of knowing* the answer.
4. be capable of	She *is capable of memorizing* long lists of words.	12. be responsible for	Who *is responsible for repairing* the roads?
5. be committed to	Dr. Pak *is committed to improving* medical care in rural areas.	13. be tired of / from	He *was tired of running*. He *was tired from running*.*
6. be devoted to	*They are devoted to helping* the poor.	14. be used to	She *is used to working* weekends.
7. be excited about	She *is excited about starting* college.	15. be worried about	The driver *was worried about getting* a traffic ticket.
8. be guilty of	He *was guilty of lying* to the judge.		

He was tired **of running.* = He doesn't want to run anymore.
 *He was tired **from** running.* = He was tired because of running.

My husband *takes care of weeding* our garden.

CHAPTER 15

Gerunds and Infinitives, Part 2

15-1 Infinitive of Purpose: *In Order To*

(a) He came here *in order to study* English. (b) He came here *to study* English.	*In order to* is used to express *purpose*. It answers the question "Why?" *In order* is often omitted, as in (b).
(c) *INCORRECT:* He came here ~~for studying~~ English. (d) *INCORRECT:* He came here ~~for to study~~ English. (e) *INCORRECT:* He came here ~~for study~~ English.	To express purpose, use (*in order*) *to*, not *for*, with a verb.*
(f) I went to the store *for* some bread. (g) I went to the store *to buy* some bread.	*For* can be used to express purpose, but it is a preposition and is followed by a noun object, as in (f).

*Exception: The phrase *be used for* expresses the typical or general purpose of a thing. In this case, the preposition *for* is followed by a gerund: *A saw **is used for cutting** wood.* Also possible: *A saw **is used to cut** wood.*
   However, to talk about a particular thing and a particular situation, *be used* + *an infinitive* is generally used: *A chain saw **was used to cut** (NOT *for cutting*) down the old oak tree.*

15-2 Adjectives Followed by Infinitives

(a) We *were sorry to hear* the bad news. (b) I *was surprised to see* Ted at the meeting.	Certain adjectives can be immediately followed by infinitives, as in (a) and (b). In general, these adjectives describe a person (or persons), not a thing. Many of these adjectives describe a person's feelings or attitudes.

Common adjectives followed by infinitives

glad to (do it)	sorry to*	ready to	careful to	surprised to*
happy to	sad to*	prepared to	hesitant to	amazed to*
pleased to*	upset to*	anxious to	reluctant to	astonished to*
delighted to	disappointed to*	eager to	afraid to	shocked to*
content to		willing to		stunned to*
relieved to	embarrassed to	motivated to	certain to	
lucky to	proud to	determined to	likely to	
fortunate to	ashamed to		unlikely to	
excited to				

*The expressions with asterisks are usually followed by infinitive phrases with verbs such as *see, learn, discover, find out, hear.*

15-3 Using Infinitives with *Too* and *Enough*

COMPARE:	*Too* can be followed by an infinitive, as in (a). In the speaker's mind, the use of *too* implies a negative result.
(a) That box is *too heavy* for Bob to lift.	In (a): *too heavy* = It is *impossible* for Bob to lift that box.
(b) That box is *very heavy*, but Bob can lift it.	In (b): *very heavy* = It is *possible but difficult* for Bob to lift that box.
(c) I am *strong enough to lift* that box. I can lift it.	*Enough* can also be followed by an infinitive. Note the following:
(d) I have *enough strength to lift* that box.	• *Enough* follows the adjective, as in (c).
(e) I have *strength enough to lift* that box.	• Usually *enough* precedes a noun, as in (d). • In formal English, it may follow a noun, as in (e).

15-4 Passive Infinitives and Gerunds: Present

(a) I didn't *expect to be asked* to his party.	PASSIVE INFINITIVE: *to be* + *past participle*
	In (a): *to be asked* is a passive infinitive.
	The understood *by*-phrase is *by him*: *I didn't expect to be asked to his party (by him).*
(b) I *appreciated being asked* to his party.	PASSIVE GERUND: *being* + *past participle*
	In (b): *being asked* is a passive gerund.
	The understood *by*-phrase is *by him*: *I appreciated being asked to his party (by him).*

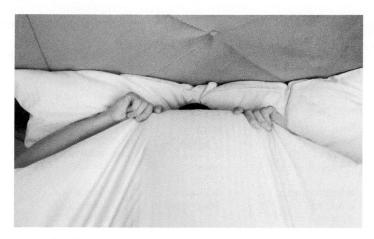

Ben didn't *appreciate* **being told** to get out of bed so early.

15-5 Past Forms of Infinitives and Gerunds: Active and Passive

SIMPLE	PAST ACTIVE	PAST PASSIVE	Past infinitives and gerunds use a form of **have** + past participle.
to tell telling	*to have told* *having told*	*to have been told* *having been told*	

(a) Tim appeared *to have told* his wife about his job promotion.	PAST INFINITIVE: **to have** + *past participle* The event expressed in past phrases happened before the time of the main verb. The meaning in (a): It appeared that Tim had told his wife about his job promotion.
(b) Tim's wife was happy *to have been told* immediately about his job promotion.	PAST PASSIVE INFINITIVE: **to have been** + *past participle* The meaning in (b): Tim's wife was happy that she had been told immediately about his job promotion.
(c) He mentioned *having told* his wife immediately about his job promotion.	PAST GERUND: **having** + *past participle* The meaning in (c): He mentioned that he had told his wife immediately about his job promotion.
(d) She appreciated *having been told* immediately about his job promotion.	PAST PASSIVE GERUND: **having been** + *past participle* The meaning in (d): She appreciated that she had been told immediately about his job promotion.
(e) Tim mentioned *telling* his wife. Tim mentioned *having told* his wife. (f) She was happy *to be told*. She was happy *to have been told*.	Use of the past infinitive or gerund emphasizes that something occurred in the past, prior to another event. In practice, however, there is little difference in meaning between the simple and past forms, as in (e) and (f).

15-6 Using Gerunds or Passive Infinitives Following *Need*

(a) I *need to paint* my house. (b) John *needs to be told* the truth.	Usually an infinitive follows **need**, as in (a) and (b).
(c) My house *needs painting*. (d) My house *needs to be painted*.	In certain circumstances, a gerund may follow **need**, as in (c). In this case, the gerund carries a passive meaning. Usually the situations involve fixing or improving something. Examples (c) and (d) have the same meaning.

15-7 Using Verbs of Perception

(a) I *saw* my friend *run* down the street. (b) I *saw* my friend *running* down the street. (c) I *heard* the rain *fall* on the roof. (d) I *heard* the rain *falling* on the roof.	Certain verbs of perception are followed by either *the simple form** or *the -ing form*** of a verb. Examples (a) and (b) have essentially the same meaning, except that the *-ing* form emphasizes the idea of "while." In (b): I saw my friend while she was running down the street.
(e) When I walked into the apartment, I *heard* my roommate *singing* in the shower. (f) I *heard* a famous opera star *sing* at the concert last night.	Sometimes (not always) there is a clear difference between using the simple form or the *-ing* form. The use of the *-ing* form gives the idea that an activity is already in progress when it is perceived, as in (e): The singing was in progress when I first heard it. In (f): I heard the singing from beginning to end. It was not in progress when I first heard it.

Verbs of perception followed by the simple form or the *-ing* form

see	look at	hear	feel	smell
notice	observe	listen to		
watch				

*The simple form of a verb = the infinitive form without *to*. INCORRECT: I saw my friend ~~to~~ run down the street.
**The *-ing* form is the present participle of the verb.

15-8 Using the Simple Form After *Let* and *Help*

(a) My father *lets* me *drive* his car. (b) I *let* my friend *borrow* my bike. (c) *Let's go* to a movie.	**Let** is followed by the simple form of a verb, not an infinitive. INCORRECT: My father lets me ~~to~~ drive his car.
(d) My brother *helped* me *wash* my car. (e) My brother *helped* me *to wash* my car.	**Help** is often followed by the simple form of a verb, as in (d). Although less common, an infinitive is also possible, as in (e). Both (d) and (e) are correct.

I *let* my friend *borrow* my bike,
and now it has a flat tire.

15-9 Using Causative Verbs: *Make, Have, Get*

(a) I *made* my brother *carry* my suitcase.	*Make*, *have*, and *get* can be used to express the idea that "X" causes "Y" to do something. When they are used as causative verbs, their meanings are similar but not identical.
(b) I *had* my brother *carry* my suitcase.	
(c) I *got* my brother *to carry* my suitcase.	

Simple form: X *makes* Y *do* something. Simple form: X *has* Y *do* something. Infinitive: X *gets* Y *to do* something.	In (a): My brother had no choice. I insisted that he carry my suitcase. In (b): My brother carried my suitcase because I asked him to. In (c): I managed to persuade my brother to carry my suitcase.

Causative *Make*

(d) Mrs. Lee *made* her son *clean* his room. (e) Sad movies *make* me *cry*.	Causative *make* is followed by the simple form of a verb, not an infinitive. *INCORRECT*: She made him ~~to~~ clean his room. *Make* gives the idea that "X" **gives** "Y" **no choice**. In (d): Mrs. Lee's son had no choice.

Causative *Have*

(f) I *had* the plumber *repair* the leak. (g) Jane *had* the waiter *bring* her some tea.	Causative *have* is followed by the simple form of a verb, not an infinitive. *INCORRECT*: I had him ~~to~~ repair the leak. *Have* gives the idea that "X" **requests** "Y" to do something. In (f): The plumber repaired the leak because I asked him to.

Causative *Get*

(h) The students *got* the teacher *to dismiss* class early. (i) Jack *got* his friends *to play* soccer with him after school.	Causative *get* is followed by an infinitive. *Get* gives the idea that "X" **persuades** "Y" to do something. In (h): The students managed to persuade the teacher to let them leave early.

Passive Causatives

(j) I *had* my watch *repaired* (by someone). (k) I *got* my watch *repaired* (by someone).	The past participle is used after *have* and *get* to give a passive meaning. In this case, there is usually little or no difference in meaning between *have* and *get*. In (j) and (k): I caused my watch to be repaired by someone.

15-10 Using a Possessive to Modify a Gerund

— We came to class late. Mr. Lee complained about that fact. (a) FORMAL: Mr. Lee complained about *our coming* to class late. (b) INFORMAL: Mr. Lee complained about *us coming* to class late.	In formal English, a possessive adjective (e.g., *our*) is used to modify a gerund, as in (a). In informal English, the object form of a pronoun (e.g., *us*) is frequently used, as in (b).
(c) FORMAL: Mr. Lee complained about *Mary's coming* to class late. (d) INFORMAL: Mr. Lee complained about *Mary coming* to class late.	In formal English, a possessive noun (e.g., *Mary's*) is used to modify a gerund. As in (d), the possessive form is often not used in informal English.

CHAPTER 16 Coordinating Conjunctions

16-1 Parallel Structure

One use of a conjunction is to connect words or phrases that have the same grammatical function in a sentence. This use of conjunctions is called "parallel structure." The conjunctions used in this pattern are **and, but, or**, and **nor**. These words are called "coordinating conjunctions."

(a) *Steve* and his *friend* are coming to dinner.	In (a): *noun + **and** + noun*
(b) Susan *raised* her hand **and** *snapped* her fingers.	In (b): *verb + **and** + verb*
(c) He *is waving* his arms **and** *(is) shouting* at us.	In (c): *verb + **and** + verb* (The second auxiliary may be omitted if it is the same as the first auxiliary.)
(d) These shoes are *old* **but** *comfortable*.	In (d): *adjective + **but** + adjective*
(e) He wants *to watch* TV **or** *(to) listen* to some music.	In (e): *infinitive + **or** + infinitive* (The second *to* is usually omitted.)

16-2 Parallel Structure: Using Commas

(a) **Steve** and **Joe** are in class.	No commas are used when *and* connects **two** parts of a parallel structure, as in (a).
(b) *INCORRECT PUNCTUATION:* Steve, and Joe are in class.	
(c) **Steve, Joe** and **Rita** are in class.	When *and* connects **three or more** parts of a parallel structure, a comma is used between the first items in the series.
(d) **Steve, Joe,** and **Rita** are in class.	A comma may also be used before *and*, as in (d) and (f). The use of this comma is optional (i.e., the writer can choose).*
(e) **Steve, Joe, Rita, Jan** and **Kim** are in class.	
(f) **Steve, Joe, Rita, Jan,** and **Kim** are in class.	NOTE: A comma often represents a pause in speech.

*The purpose of punctuation is to make writing clear for readers. This chart and others in this chapter describe the usual use of commas in parallel structures. Sometimes commas are required according to convention (i.e., the expected use by educated language users). Sometimes use of commas is a stylistic choice made by the experienced writer.

16-3 Punctuation for Independent Clauses; Connecting Them with *And* and *But*

(a) It was raining hard. There was a strong wind.	Example (a) contains two *independent clauses* (i.e., two complete sentences).
(b) INCORRECT PUNCTUATION: It was raining hard, there was a strong wind.	PUNCTUATION: A period,* NOT A COMMA, is used to separate two independent clauses.
(c) It was raining hard; there was a strong wind.	A semicolon may be used in place of a period. Semicolons are used between two *closely related* ideas.
(d) It was raining hard, *and* there was a strong wind. (e) It was raining hard. *And* there was a strong wind. (f) It was raining hard *and* there was a strong wind. (g) It was late, *but* he didn't care. (h) It was late. *But* he didn't care.	*And* and *but* (coordinating conjunctions) are often used to connect two independent clauses. PUNCTUATION: Usually a comma immediately precedes the conjunction, as in (d) and (g). In informal writing, a writer might choose to begin a sentence with a conjunction, as in (e) and (h). In a very short sentence, a writer might choose to omit the comma in front of *and*, as in (f). (Omitting the comma in front of *but* is rare.)

*In British English, a period is called a "full stop."

16-4 Paired Conjunctions: *Both ... And; Not Only ... But Also; Either ... Or; Neither ... Nor*

(a) *Both* my mother *and* my sister *are* here.	Two subjects connected by *both ... and* take a plural verb, as in (a).
(b) *Not only* my mother *but also* my sister *is* here. (c) *Not only* my sister *but also* my parents *are* here. (d) *Neither* my mother *nor* my sister *is* here. (e) *Neither* my sister *nor* my parents *are* here.	When two subjects are connected by *not only ... but also*, *either ... or*, or *neither ... nor*, the subject that is closer to the verb determines whether the verb is singular or plural. *Not only ... but also* is used for emphasis or to indicate surprise. It should be used sparingly.
(f) The research project will take *both* time *and* money. (g) Sue saw *not only* a fox in the woods *but also* a bear. (h) I'll take *either* chemistry *or* physics next quarter. (i) That book is *neither* interesting *nor* accurate.	Notice the parallel structure in the examples. The same grammatical form should follow each part of the paired conjunctions.*
	In (f): *both* + noun + *and* + noun In (g): *not only* + noun + *but also* + noun In (h): *either* + noun + *or* + noun In (i): *neither* + adjective + *nor* + adjective NOTE: Paired conjunctions are usually used for emphasis; they draw attention to both parts of the parallel structure.

*Paired conjunctions are also called "correlative conjunctions."

CHAPTER 17 Adverb Clauses

17-1 Introduction

Adverb clauses are used to show relationships between ideas. They show relationships of *time, cause and effect, contrast,* and *condition.*

adverb clause ⌐ main clause⌐ (a) *When the phone rang,* the baby woke up. (b) The baby woke up *when the phone rang*.	In (a) and (b): ***when the phone rang*** is an adverb clause of time. Examples (a) and (b) have the same meaning. PUNCTUATION: When an adverb clause precedes a main clause, as in (a), a comma is used to separate the clauses. When the adverb clause follows, as in (b), usually no comma is used.
(c) *Because he was sleepy,* he went to bed. (d) He went to bed *because he was sleepy*.	In (c) and (d), ***because*** introduces an adverb clause that shows a cause-and-effect relationship.
(e) *INCORRECT:* When we were in New York. We saw several plays. (f) *INCORRECT:* He went to bed. Because he was sleepy.	Adverb clauses are dependent clauses. They cannot stand alone as a sentence in written English. They must be connected to a main (or independent) clause.*

Summary list of words used to introduce adverb clauses**

TIME		CAUSE AND EFFECT	CONTRAST	CONDITION
after	by the time (that)	because	even though	if
before	once	now that	although	unless
when	as/so long as	since	though	only if
while	whenever			whether or not
as	every time (that)		DIRECT CONTRAST	even if
as soon as	the first time (that)		while	in case
since	the last time (that)			
until	the next time (that)			

*See Chart 12-1, p. 63, for the definition of dependent and independent clauses.

**Words that introduce adverb clauses are called "subordinating conjunctions."

17-2 Using Adverb Clauses to Show Time Relationships

after *	(a) *After* she graduates, she will get a job. (b) *After* she (had) graduated, she got a job.	A present tense, NOT a future tense, is used in an adverb clause of time, as in (a) and (c). (See Chart 3-3, p. 19, for tense usage in future time clauses.)
before *	(c) I will leave *before* he comes. (d) I (had) left *before* he came.	
when	(e) *When* I arrived, he *was talking* on the phone. (f) *When* I got there, he *had* already *left*. (g) *When* it began to rain, I *stood* under a tree. (h) *When* I was in Chicago, I *visited* the museums. (i) *When* I see him tomorrow, I *will ask* him.	***when*** = at that time Notice the different time relationships expressed by the tenses.
while *as*	(j) *While* I was walking home, it began to rain. (k) *As* I was walking home, it began to rain.	***while, as*** = during that time
by the time	(l) *By the time* he arrived, we *had* already *left*. (m) *By the time* he comes, we *will have* already *left*.	***by the time*** = one event is completed before another event Notice the use of the past perfect and future perfect in the main clause.
since	(n) I *haven't seen* him *since* he left this morning. (o) I*'ve known* her *ever since* I was a child.	***since*** = from that time to the present In (o): ***ever*** adds emphasis. NOTE: The present perfect is used in the main clause.
until *till*	(p) We stayed there *until* we finished our work. (q) We stayed there *till* we finished our work.	***until, till*** = to that time and then no longer (***Till*** is used more in speaking than in writing; it is generally not used in formal English.)
as soon as *once*	(r) *As soon as* it stops raining, we will leave. (s) *Once* it stops raining, we will leave.	***as soon as, once*** = when one event happens, another event happens soon afterward
as long as *so long as*	(t) I will never speak to him again *as long as* I live. (u) I will never speak to him again *so long as* I live.	***as long as, so long as*** = during all that time, from beginning to end
whenever *every time*	(v) *Whenever* I see her, I say hello. (w) *Every time* I see her, I say hello.	***whenever*** = every time
the first time *the last time* *the next time*	(x) *The first time* (that) I went to New York, I went to a Broadway show. (y) I saw two plays *the last time* (that) I went to New York. (z) *The next time* (that) I go to New York, I'm going to see a ballet.	Adverb clauses can be introduced by: the { first / second / third, etc. / last / next / etc. } time (that)

After and *before* are commonly used in the following expressions:

shortly *after*   **shortly** *before*
a short time *after*   **a short time** *before*
a little while *after*   **a little while** *before*
not long *after*   **not long** *before*
soon *after*

17-3 Using Adverb Clauses to Show Cause and Effect

because	(a) *Because* he was sleepy, he went to bed. (b) He went to bed *because* he was sleepy.	An adverb clause may precede or follow the independent clause. Notice the punctuation in (a) and (b). Be sure to identify the correct cause and effect. INCORRECT: Because he went to bed, he was sleepy.
now that	(c) *Now that* I've finished the semester, I'm going to rest a few days and then take a trip. (d) Jack lost his job. *Now that* he's unemployed, he can't pay his bills.	***Now that*** means "because now." In (c): ***Now that I've finished the semester*** means "because the semester is now over." NOTE: ***Now that*** is used with the present, present perfect, or future tenses.
since	(e) *Since* Monday is a holiday, we don't have to go to work. (f) *Since* you're a good cook and I'm not, you should cook the dinner.	When ***since*** is used to mean "because," it expresses a known cause; it means "because it is a fact that" or "given that it is true that." Cause-and-effect sentences with ***since*** say, "Given the fact that X is true, Y is the result." In (e): "Given the fact that Monday is a holiday, we don't have to go to work."
	(g) *Since* I came here, I have met many people.	NOTE: ***Since*** has two meanings. One is "because." It is also used in time clauses, as in (g). See Chart 17-2.

17-4 Expressing Contrast (Unexpected Result): Using *Even Though*

(a) *Because* the weather was cold, I *didn't go* swimming. (b) *Even though* the weather was cold, I *went* swimming. (c) *Because* I wasn't tired, I *didn't go* to bed. (d) *Even though* I wasn't tired, I *went* to bed.	***Because*** is used to express expected results. ***Even though*** is used to express unexpected results.* NOTE: Like ***because***, ***even though*** introduces an adverb clause.

Although and *though* have basically the same meaning and use as *even though*. See Chart 19-7, p. 102, for information on the use of *although* and *though*.

17-5 Showing Direct Contrast: *While*

(a) Mary is rich, *while* John is poor. (b) John is poor, *while* Mary is rich. (c) *While* John is poor, Mary is rich. (d) *While* Mary is rich, John is poor.	***While*** is used to show direct contrast: "this" is exactly the opposite of "that."* Examples (a), (b), (c), and (d) all have the same meaning. Note the use of the comma in (a) and (b): In using ***while*** for direct contrast, a comma is often used even if the ***while***-clause comes second (unlike the punctuation of most other adverb clauses).
COMPARE: (e) The phone rang *while* I was studying.	REMINDER: ***While*** is also used in time clauses and means "during that time," as in (e). See Chart 17-2.

Whereas can have the same meaning and use as ***while***, but it occurs mostly in formal written English and occurs with considerably less frequency than ***while***: *Mary is rich,* ***whereas*** *John is poor.*

17-6 Expressing Conditions in Adverb Clauses: *If*-Clauses

(a) *If* it *rains* tomorrow, I *will take* my umbrella.	*If*-clauses (also called "adverb clauses of condition") present possible conditions. The main clause expresses RESULTS. In (a): POSSIBLE CONDITION = *it may rain tomorrow* RESULT = *I will take my umbrella* A present tense, not a future tense, is used in an *if*-clause even though the verb in the *if*-clause may refer to a future event or situation, as in (a).*

Words that introduce adverb clauses of condition (*if-clauses*)

if	even if	unless
whether or not	in case	only if

*See Chapter 20 for uses of other verb forms in sentences with *if*-clauses.

17-7 Shortened *If*-Clauses

(a) Are you a student? *If so / If you are,* the ticket is half-price. *If not / If you aren't,* the ticket is full price. (b) It's a popular concert. Do you have a ticket? *If so / If you do,* you're lucky. *If not / If you don't,* you're out of luck.	When an *if*-clause refers to the idea in the sentence immediately before it, it is sometimes shortened. In (a): ***If so / If you are*** = If you are a student ***If not / If you aren't*** = If you aren't a student In (b): ***If so / If you do*** = If you have a ticket ***If not / If you don't*** = If you don't have a ticket

17-8 Adverb Clauses of Condition: Using *Whether Or Not* and *Even If*

Whether or not

(a) I'm going to go swimming tomorrow *whether or not it is cold.* OR *whether it is cold or not.*	***Whether or not*** expresses the idea that neither this condition nor that condition matters; the result will be the same. In (a): "If it is cold, I'm going swimming. If it is not cold, I'm going swimming. I don't care about the temperature. It doesn't matter."

Even if

(b) I have decided to go swimming tomorrow. *Even if the weather is cold,* I'm going to go swimming.	Sentences with ***even if*** are close in meaning to those with ***whether or not***. ***Even if*** gives the idea that a particular condition does not matter. The result will not change.

17-9 Adverb Clauses of Condition: Using *In Case*

(a) I'll be at my uncle's house *in case you (should) need to reach me.*	***In case*** expresses the idea that something probably won't happen, but it might. ***In case*** means "if by chance this should happen." NOTE: Using ***should*** in an adverb clause emphasizes the speaker's uncertainty that something will happen.

17-10 Adverb Clauses of Condition: Using *Unless*

(a) I'll go swimming tomorrow *unless it's cold.* (b) I'll go swimming tomorrow *if it isn't cold.*	***unless = if … not*** In (a): *unless it's cold* means "if it isn't cold." Examples (a) and (b) have the same meaning.

17-11 Adverb Clauses of Condition: Using *Only If*

(a) The picnic will be canceled *only if it rains.* If it's windy, we'll go on the picnic. If it's cold, we'll go on the picnic. If it's damp and foggy, we'll go on the picnic. If it's unbearably hot, we'll go on the picnic.	***Only if*** expresses the idea that there is only one condition that will cause a particular result.
(b) *Only if it rains will the picnic be canceled.*	When ***only if*** begins a sentence, the subject and verb of the main clause are inverted, as in (b).* This is a less common usage. No commas are used.

*Other subordinating conjunctions and prepositional phrases preceded by ***only*** at the beginning of a sentence require subject-verb inversion in the main clause:
> ***Only when*** the teacher dismisses us ***can we stand*** and ***leave*** the room.
> ***Only after*** the phone rang ***did I realize*** that I had fallen asleep in my chair.
> ***Only in*** my hometown ***do I feel*** at ease.

CHAPTER 18

Reduction of Adverb Clauses to Modifying Adverbial Phrases

18-1 Introduction

(a) Adverb clause:	*While I was walking* to class, I ran into an old friend.	In Chapter 13, we discussed changing adjective clauses to modifying phrases. (See Chart 13-11, p. 74.) Some adverb clauses may also be changed to modifying phrases, and the ways in which the changes are made are the same:
(b) Modifying phrase:	*While **walking** to class,* I ran into an old friend.	
(c) Adverb clause:	*Before **I left** for work,* I ate breakfast.	• If there is a **be** form of the verb, omit the subject of the dependent clause and **be** verb, as in (b). OR
(d) Modifying phrase:	*Before **leaving** for work,* I ate breakfast.	• If there is no **be** form of a verb, omit the subject and change the verb to **-ing**, as in (d).
(e) Change possible:	*While **I** was sitting in class,* I fell asleep. *While sitting in class,* I fell asleep.	An adverb clause can be changed to a modifying phrase **only when the subject of the adverb clause and the subject of the main clause are the same.**
(f) Change possible:	*While **Ann** was sitting in class, **she** fell asleep.* (clause) *While sitting in class, **Ann** fell asleep.*	A *modifying adverbial phrase* that is the reduction of an adverb clause *modifies the subject* of the main clause.
(g) No change possible:	*While **the teacher** was lecturing to the class, I fell asleep.**	No reduction (i.e., change) is possible if the subjects of the adverb clause and the main clause are different, as in (g).
(h) INCORRECT:	~~While watching TV last night,~~ the phone rang.	In (h): *While watching* is called a "dangling modifier" or a "dangling participle," i.e., a modifier that is incorrectly "hanging alone" without an appropriate noun or pronoun subject to modify.

While lecturing to the class, I fell asleep* means "While **I was lecturing to the class, **I** fell asleep."

18-2 Changing Time Clauses to Modifying Adverbial Phrases

(a)	Clause:	*Since Maria came* to this country, she has made many friends.	Adverb clauses beginning with **after**, **before**, **when**,* **while**, and **since** can be changed to modifying adverbial phrases.
(b)	Phrase:	*Since coming* to this country, Maria has made many friends.	
(c)	Clause:	*When Tyrell cooks*, he uses a lot of spices.	
(d)	Phrase:	*When cooking*, Tyrell uses a lot of spices.	
(e)	Clause:	*After he (had) finished* his homework, Peter went to bed.	In (e): There is no difference in meaning between *After he finished* and *After he had finished*. (See Chart 2-8, p. 15.)
(f)	Phrase:	*After finishing* his homework, Peter went to bed.	In (f) and (g): There is no difference in meaning between *After finishing* and *After having finished*.
(g)	Phrase:	*After having finished* his homework, Peter went to bed.	
(h)	Phrase:	Peter went to bed *after finishing* his homework.	The modifying adverbial phrase may follow the main clause, as in (h).

When can also mean "upon." If it has this meaning, it cannot be reduced to a phrase. See Chart 18-5.

18-3 Expressing the Idea of "During the Same Time" in Modifying Adverbial Phrases

(a)	*While I was walking* down the street, *I* ran into an old friend.	Sometimes **while** is omitted, but the **-ing** phrase at the beginning of the sentence gives the same meaning (i.e., "during the same time").
(b)	*While walking* down the street, *I* ran into an old friend.	
(c)	*Walking* down the street, *I* ran into an old friend.	Examples (a), (b), and (c) have the same meaning.

While George was resting on the beach, *he* fell asleep.
Resting on the beach, *George* fell asleep.

18-4 Expressing Cause and Effect in Modifying Adverbial Phrases

(a) *Because she needed* some money to buy a book, *Sue* went to a cash machine.	Often an *-ing* phrase at the beginning of a sentence gives the meaning of "because."
(b) *Needing* some money to buy a book, *Sue* went to a cash machine.	Examples (a) and (b) have the same meaning.
(c) *Because he lacked* the necessary qualifications, *he* was not considered for the job.	*Because* is not included in a modifying phrase. It is omitted, but the resulting phrase expresses a cause-and-effect relationship, as in (b) and (d).
(d) *Lacking* the necessary qualifications, *he* was not considered for the job.	
(e) *Having seen* that movie before, *I don't want* to go again.	*Having* + *past participle* gives the meaning not only of "because" but also of "before."
(f) *Having seen* that movie before, *I didn't want* to go again.	
(g) *Because he is* a doctor, Oskar often gets calls in the middle of the night.	A form of *be* in the adverb clause may be changed to *being*. The use of *being* makes the cause-and-effect relationship clear.
(h) *Being* a doctor, Oskar often gets calls in the middle of the night.	Examples (i), (j), and (k) have the same meaning.
(i) *Because she was unable* to afford a car, *she* bought a bike.	
(j) *Being unable* to afford a car, *she* bought a bike.	
(k) *Unable* to afford a car, *she* bought a bike.	

18-5 Using *Upon* + *-ing* in Modifying Adverbial Phrases

(a) *Upon reaching* the age of 18, I can get my driver's license.	Modifying adverbial phrases beginning with *upon* + *-ing* can have the same meaning as adverb clauses introduced by *when*.
(b) *When I reach* the age of 18, I can get my driver's license.	Examples (a) and (b) have the same meaning.
(c) *On reaching* the age of 18, I can get my driver's license.	*Upon* can be shortened to *on*. Examples (a), (b), and (c) all have the same meaning.

CHAPTER 19

Connectives That Express Cause and Effect, Contrast, and Condition

<table>
<tr><td colspan="2">19-1 Introduction</td></tr>
<tr><td colspan="2">Connectives can express cause/effect, contrast, and condition. They can be adverb-clause words, transitions, conjunctions, or prepositions. In Chapter 17 you studied adverb-clause words to express these ideas. In this chapter you will also look at transitions, conjunctions, and prepositions.</td></tr>
<tr>
<td>(a) Because Julian felt sick, he left work early.
(b) Even though Julian is afraid of doctors, he decided to make an appointment.</td>
<td>The connectives in (a) and (b) are adverb-clause words.</td>
</tr>
<tr>
<td>(c) Julian had a rash and fever. Consequently, the doctor ran tests.
(d) The doctor ran tests. However, she found nothing serious.</td>
<td>The connectives in (c) and (d) are transitions.</td>
</tr>
<tr>
<td>(e) Julian wasn't seriously ill, but his doctor told him to rest anyway.
(f) Julian wasn't well, so his doctor told him to rest.</td>
<td>The connectives in (e) and (f) are conjunctions.</td>
</tr>
<tr>
<td>(g) Due to his illness, Julian missed several days of work.
(h) He stayed home from work because of his illness.</td>
<td>The connectives in (g) and (h) are prepositions.</td>
</tr>
</table>

	Adverb-Clause Words		Transitions	Conjunctions	Prepositions
CAUSE AND EFFECT	because since now that	so (that)	therefore consequently	so	because of due to
CONTRAST	even though although though	while	however nevertheless nonetheless on the other hand	but (… anyway) yet (… still)	despite in spite of
CONDITION	if unless only if even if whether or not	in case	otherwise	or (else)	

19-2 Using *Because Of* and *Due To*

(a) *Because the weather was cold,* we stayed home.	*Because* introduces an adverb clause; it is followed by a subject and a verb, as in (a).
(b) *Because of the cold weather,* we stayed home. (c) *Due to the cold weather,* we stayed home.	*Because of* and *due to* are phrasal prepositions; they are followed by a noun object, as in (b) and (c).
(d) *Due to the fact that the weather was cold,* we stayed home.	Sometimes (usually in more formal writing) *due to* is followed by a noun clause introduced by *the fact that*.
(e) We stayed home *because of the cold weather.* We stayed home *due to the cold weather.* We stayed home *due to the fact that the weather was cold.*	Like adverb clauses, these phrases can also follow the main clause, as in (e).

19-3 Cause and Effect: Using *Therefore, Consequently,* and *So*

(a) Al failed the test because he didn't study. (b) Al didn't study. *Therefore,* he failed the test. (c) Al didn't study. *Consequently,* he failed the test.	Examples (a), (b), and (c) have the same meaning. *Therefore* and *consequently* mean "as a result." In grammar, they are called *transitions* (or *conjunctive adverbs*). Transitions connect the ideas between two sentences. They are used most commonly in formal written English and rarely in spoken English.

(d) Al didn't study. *Therefore,* he failed the test.
(e) Al didn't study. He*, therefore,* failed the test.
(f) Al didn't study. He failed the test*, therefore.*
 	
POSITIONS OF A TRANSITION:
 	
transition + **S** + **V** (+ rest of sentence)
   S + *transition* + **V** (+ rest of sentence)
   S + **V** (+ rest of sentence) + *transition*
	A transition occurs in the second of two related sentences.
	
	Notice the patterns and punctuation in the examples. A period (NOT a comma) is used at the end of the first sentence.*
	
	The transition has several positions in the second sentence. It is separated from the rest of the sentence by commas.

(g) Al didn't study*, so* he failed the test.	In (g): *So* is used as a *conjunction* between two independent clauses. It has the same meaning as *therefore*. *So* is common in both formal written and spoken English. A comma usually precedes *so* when it connects two sentences, as in (g).

*A semicolon is also possible in this situation: *Al didn't study; therefore, he failed the test.* See the footnote to Chart 19-4.

19-4 Summary of Patterns and Punctuation

ADVERB CLAUSES	(a) *Because it was hot*, we went swimming. (b) We went swimming *because it was hot*.	An *adverb clause* may precede or follow an independent clause. PUNCTUATION: A comma is used if the adverb clause comes first.
PREPOSITIONS	(c) *Because of the hot weather*, we went swimming. (d) We went swimming *because of the hot weather*.	A *preposition* is followed by a noun object, not by a subject and verb. PUNCTUATION: A comma is usually used if the prepositional phrase precedes the subject and verb of the independent clause.
TRANSITIONS	(e) It was hot. *Therefore, we went swimming.* (f) It was hot. *We, therefore, went swimming.* (g) It was hot. *We went swimming, therefore.* (h) It was hot; *therefore, we went swimming.*	A *transition* is used with the second sentence of a pair. It shows the relationship of the second idea to the first idea. A transition is movable within the second sentence. PUNCTUATION: A semicolon (;) may be used in place of a period, as in (h).* NOTE: A period is used between the two independent clauses in (e)–(g); a comma is not possible. Commas are usually used to set the transition off from the rest of the sentence.
CONJUNCTIONS	(i) It was hot, *so we went swimming.*	A conjunction comes between two independent clauses. PUNCTUATION: Usually a comma is used immediately in front of a conjunction.

* In general, a semicolon can be used instead of a period between any two sentences that are closely related in meaning: *Peanuts are not nuts; they are beans.* Notice that a small letter, NOT a capital letter, immediately follows a semicolon.

19-5 Other Ways of Expressing Cause and Effect: *Such ... That* and *So ... That*

(a) Because the weather was nice, we went to the zoo. (b) It was *such nice weather that* we went to the zoo. (c) The weather was *so nice that* we went to the zoo.	Examples (a), (b), and (c) have the same meaning.
(d) It was *such good coffee that* I had another cup. (e) It was *such a foggy day that* we couldn't see the road.	*Such ... that* encloses a modified noun: *such + adjective + noun + that*
(f) The coffee is *so hot that* I can't drink it. (g) I'm *so hungry that* I could eat a horse. (h) She speaks *so fast that* I can't understand her. (i) He walked *so quickly that* I couldn't keep up with him.	*So ... that* encloses an adjective or adverb: *so* + { *adjective* or *adverb* } + *that*
(j) She made *so many mistakes that* she failed the exam. (k) He has *so few friends that* he is always lonely. (l) She has *so much money that* she can buy whatever she wants. (m) He had *so little trouble* with the test *that* he left 20 minutes early.	*So ... that* is used with *many, few, much,* and *little*.
(n) It was *such a good book* (that) I couldn't put it down. (o) I was *so hungry* (that) I didn't wait for dinner to eat something.	Sometimes, primarily in speaking, *that* is omitted.

19-6 Expressing Purpose: Using *So That*

(a) I turned off the TV *in order to enable my roommate to study in peace and quiet.*	***In order to*** expresses *purpose*. (See Chart 15-1, p. 83.) In (a): I turned off the TV for a purpose. The purpose was to make it possible for my roommate to study in peace and quiet. Examples (a) and (b) have the same meaning.
(b) I turned off the TV *so (that) my roommate could study in peace and quiet.*	

So That + Can or Could

(c) I'm going to cash a check *so that I can buy my textbooks.*	***So that*** also expresses *purpose*.* It expresses the same meaning as ***in order to***. The word *that* is often omitted, especially in speaking.
(d) I cashed a check *so that I could buy my textbooks.*	***So that*** is often used instead of ***in order to*** when the idea of ability is being expressed. ***Can*** is used in the adverb clause for a present/future meaning. In (c): ***so that I can buy*** = *in order to be able to buy* ***Could*** is used after ***so that*** in past sentences, as in (d).**

So That + Will / Would or Simple Present

(e) I'll take my umbrella *so that I won't get wet.*	In (e): ***so that I won't get wet*** = *in order to make sure that I won't get wet*
(f) Yesterday I took my umbrella *so that I wouldn't get wet.*	***Would*** is used in past sentences, as in (f).
(g) I'll take my umbrella *so that I don't get wet.*	In (g): It is sometimes possible to use the simple present after ***so that*** in place of ***will***; the simple present expresses a future meaning.

*Note: *In order that* has the same meaning as *so that* but is less commonly used.
   Example: *I turned off the TV **in order that** my roommate could study in peace and quiet.*
Both *so that* and *in order that* introduce adverb clauses. It is unusual but possible to put these adverb clauses at the beginning of a sentence: ***So that** my roommate could study in peace and quiet, I turned off the TV.*
Also possible but less common: the use of ***may* or ***might*** in place of ***can*** or ***could*** (e.g., *I cashed a check **so that I might** buy my textbooks.*).

He asked for help ***so that he could*** find a campsite.

19-7 Showing Contrast (Unexpected Result)

All of these sentences have the same meaning. The idea of cold weather is contrasted with the idea of going swimming. Usually if the weather is cold, one does not go swimming, so going swimming in cold weather is an "unexpected result." It is surprising that the speaker went swimming in cold weather.

ADVERB CLAUSES	*even though*	(a) ***Even though*** *it was cold,* I went swimming.
	although	(b) ***Although*** *it was cold,* I went swimming.
	though	(c) ***Though*** *it was cold,* I went swimming.*
CONJUNCTIONS	*but … anyway*	(d) It was cold, ***but*** I went swimming *(anyway)*.
	but … still	(e) It was cold, ***but*** I *(still)* went swimming.
	yet … still	(f) It was cold, ***yet*** I *(still)* went swimming.
TRANSITIONS	*nevertheless*	(g) It was cold. ***Nevertheless,*** I went swimming.
	nonetheless	(h) It was cold; ***nonetheless,*** I went swimming.
	however … still	(i) It was cold. ***However,*** I *(still)* went swimming.
PREPOSITIONS	*despite*	(j) I went swimming ***despite*** the cold weather.
	in spite of	(k) I went swimming ***in spite of*** the cold weather.
	despite the fact that	(l) I went swimming ***despite the fact that*** the weather was cold.
	in spite of the fact that	(m) I went swimming ***in spite of the fact that*** the weather was cold.

* Another way to show contrast is to put *though* at the end of the sentence: *It was cold. I went swimming, though.* The meaning is similar to *but* (e.g., *It was cold, but I went swimming.*); however, *though* is softer. This usage is very common in spoken English.

19-8 Showing Direct Contrast

All of the sentences have the same meaning: "This" is the opposite of "that."

ADVERB CLAUSES	*while*	(a) Mary is rich, ***while*** *John is poor.**
		(b) John is poor, ***while*** *Mary is rich.*
CONJUNCTIONS	*but*	(c) Mary is rich, ***but*** *John is poor.*
		(d) John is poor, ***but*** *Mary is rich.*
TRANSITIONS	*however*	(e) Mary is rich; ***however,*** *John is poor.*
		(f) John is poor; *Mary is rich,* ***however.***
	on the other hand	(g) Mary is rich. *John,* ***on the other hand,*** *is poor.*
		(h) John is poor. *Mary,* ***on the other hand,*** *is rich.*

*Sometimes a comma precedes a *while*-clause that shows direct contrast. A comma helps clarify that *while* is being used to express contrast rather than time. The use of a comma in this instance is a stylistic choice by the writer.

19-9 Expressing Conditions: Using *Otherwise* and *Or (Else)*

ADVERB CLAUSES	(a) *If* I don't eat breakfast, I get hungry. (b) You'll be late *if* you don't hurry. (c) You'll get wet *unless* you take your umbrella.	*If* and *unless* state conditions that produce certain results. (See Charts 17-6 and 17-10, pp. 93 and 94.)
TRANSITIONS	(d) I always eat breakfast. *Otherwise,* I get hungry during class. (e) You'd better hurry. *Otherwise,* you'll be late. (f) Take your umbrella. *Otherwise,* you'll get wet.	*Otherwise* expresses the idea "if the opposite is true, then there will be a certain result." In (d): *otherwise* = if I don't eat breakfast
CONJUNCTIONS	(g) I always eat breakfast, *or (else)* I get hungry during class. (h) You'd better hurry, *or (else)* you'll be late. (i) Take your umbrella, *or (else)* you'll get wet.	*Or else* and *otherwise* have the same meaning.

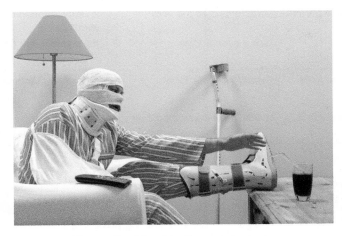

The patient had better ask for help.
Otherwise, he will spill his drink.

Conditional Sentences and Wishes

20-1 Overview of Basic Verb Forms Used in Conditional Sentences

Conditional sentences express the idea of *if ... , then ...* . These sentences can talk about real situations — facts, regularly occurring events, etc. — and unreal situations — imaginary or impossible ones.

Situation	*If*-Clause	Result Clause	Examples
REAL IN THE PRESENT REAL IN THE FUTURE	simple present	*simple form of the verb* *will* + simple form	If I *have* enough time, I *watch* TV every evening. If I *have* enough time, I *will watch* TV later on tonight.
UNREAL IN THE PRESENT / FUTURE	simple past	*would* + simple form	If I *had* enough time, I *would watch* TV now or later on.
UNREAL IN THE PAST	past perfect	*would have* + past participle	If I *had had* enough time, I *would have watched* TV yesterday.

20-2 Expressing Real Conditions in the Present or Future

(a) If I *don't eat* breakfast, I always *get* hungry during class.	In conditional sentences that express real or true, factual ideas in the present/future, the *simple present* (not the simple future) is used in the *if*-clause.
(b) If I *don't eat* breakfast tomorrow morning, I *will get* hungry during class.	The result clause has various possible verb forms. A result-clause verb can be:
(c) Water *freezes* if the temperature *reaches* 32°F/0°C.	• the *simple present,* to express a habitual activity or situation, as in (a). • the *simple future,* to express a particular activity or situation in the future, as in (b). • the s*imple present* or the *simple future,* to express an established, predictable fact or general truth, as in (c) and (d).
(d) Water *will freeze* if the temperature *reaches* 32°F/0°C.	
(e) If it *rains,* we *should stay* home. If it *rains,* I *might decide* to stay home. If it *rains,* we *can't go.* If it *rains,* we*'re going to stay* home.	The result clause can also include *modals* and *phrasal modals* such as ***should***, ***might***, ***can***, ***be going to***, as in (e).*
(f) If anyone *calls,* please *take* a message.	An imperative verb can be used in the result clause, as in (f).
(g) If anyone *should call,* please take a message.	Sometimes ***should*** is used in an *if*-clause, as in (g). It indicates a little more uncertainty than the use of the simple present, but basically the meaning of examples (f) and (g) is the same.

*See Chart 9-1, p. 44, for a list of modals and phrasal modals.

20-3 Unreal (Contrary to Fact) in the Present or Future

(a) If I *taught* this class, I *wouldn't give* tests.	In (a): Actually, I don't teach this class.
(b) If he *were* here right now, he *would help* us.	In (b): Actually, he is not here right now.
(c) If I *were* you, I *would accept* their invitation.	In (c): Actually, I am not you.
	NOTE: **Were** is used for both singular and plural subjects. **Was** (with *I, he, she, it*) is sometimes used in very informal speech: *If I **was** you, I'd accept their invitation*.
COMPARE:	In (d): The speaker wants a car but doesn't have enough money. **Would** expresses desired or predictable results.
(d) If I had enough money, I *would buy* a car.	In (e): The speaker is expressing one possible result. **could** = *would be able to*; **could** *expresses possible options*.
(e) If I had enough money, I *could buy* a car.	

20-4 Unreal (Contrary to Fact) in the Past

(a) If you *had told* me about the problem, I *would have helped* you.	In (a): Actually, you did not tell me about it.
(b) If they *had studied,* they *would have passed* the exam.	In (b): Actually, they did not study. Therefore, they failed the exam.
(c) If I *hadn't slipped* on the stairs, I *wouldn't have broken* my arm.	In (c): Actually, I slipped on the stairs. I broke my arm.
	NOTE: The auxiliary verbs are often reduced in speech. "If you'd told me, I would've helped you (or I-*duv* helped you)."*
COMPARE:	In (d): **would** expresses a desired or predictable result.
(d) If I had had enough money, I *would have bought* a car.	In (e): **could** expresses a possible option. **could have bought** = *would have been able to buy*
(e) If I had had enough money, I *could have bought* a car.	

*In casual, informal speech, some native speakers sometimes use **would have** in an *if*-clause: *If you **would've told** me about the problem, I would've helped you*. This verb form usage is generally considered to be grammatically incorrect in standard English, but it occurs fairly commonly.

If Daniel *hadn't drunk* so much coffee, he *would have felt* more relaxed.

20-5 Using Progressive Verb Forms in Conditional Sentences

Notice the use of progressive verb forms in these examples. Even in conditional sentences, progressive verb forms are used in progressive situations.

(a)	Real Situation:	It *is raining* right now, so I *will not go* for a walk.
(b)	Conditional Statement:	If it *were not raining* right now, I *would go* for a walk.
(c)	Real Situation:	It *was raining* yesterday afternoon, so I *did not go* for a walk.
(d)	Conditional Statement:	If it *had not been raining*, I *would have gone* for a walk.

20-6 Using "Mixed Time" in Conditional Sentences

Frequently the time in the *if*-clause and the time in the result clause are different: one clause may be in the present and the other in the past. Notice that past and present times are mixed in these sentences.

		past / present
(a)	Real Situation:	I *did not eat* breakfast *several hours ago*, so I *am* hungry *now*.
(b)	Conditional Statement:	If I *had eaten* breakfast *several hours ago*, I *would not be* hungry *now*.
(c)	Real Situation:	present / past He *is not* a good student. He *did not study* for the test *yesterday*.
(d)	Conditional Statement:	present / past If he *were* a good student, he *would have studied* for the test *yesterday*.

20-7 Omitting *If*

(a) *Were I* you, I wouldn't do that. (b) *Had I known*, I would have told you. (c) *Should anyone call*, please take a message.	With *were, had* (past perfect), and *should*, sometimes *if* is omitted, and the subject and verb are inverted. In (a): *Were I you* = if I were you In (b): *Had I known* = if I had known In (c): *Should anyone call* = if anyone should call

Had he known that he would become
so frustrated, he wouldn't have
started the project.

20-8 Implied Conditions

(a) I *would have gone* with you, *but I had to study*. (b) I never *would have succeeded* without your help.	Often the *if*-clause is implied, not stated. Conditional verbs are still used in the result clause. In (a): the implied condition = *if I hadn't had to study* In (b): the implied condition = *if you hadn't helped me*
(c) She ran; *otherwise*, she *would have missed* her bus.	Conditional verbs are frequently used following **otherwise**. In (c), the implied *if*-clause = *if she had not run*

20-9 Wishes About the Present and Past

Wish is used when the speaker wants reality to be different, to be exactly the opposite, but it isn't.

	"True" Statement	Verb Form Following *Wish*	*Wish* can be followed by a noun clause (see Chart 12-5, p. 65). Past verb forms, similar to those in conditional sentences, are used in the noun clause.
A WISH ABOUT THE PRESENT	(a) I *don't know* French. (b) It *is raining* right now. (c) I *can't speak* Japanese.	I wish (that) I *knew* French. I wish it *weren't raining* right now. I wish I *could speak* Japanese.	To make a wish about the present, a past verb form is used, as in (a)–(c).
A WISH ABOUT THE PAST	(d) John *didn't come*. (e) Mary *couldn't come*.	I wish John *had come*.* I wish Mary *could have come*.	In (d), the past perfect (**had come**) is used to make a wish about the past.
(f) I *wish* I *could* come. (It's not possible. I can't come.) (g) I *hope* I *can* come. (It's a possibility. Maybe I can come.)			Note the difference between **wish** and **hope**. **Wish** is used for unreal, contrary-to-fact situations. **Hope** is used for real or possible situations.

*You may hear *I wish Josh would have come*. This is incorrect in formal English.

20-10 Wishes About the Future; Use of *Wish + Would*

(a) He *isn't going to be* here next week. I wish he *were going to be* here next week. (b) She *can't come* tomorrow. I wish she *could come* tomorrow. (c) She *won't tell you*. I wish she *would tell you*. (d) I wish I *could go* with you.	Wishes about the future can be expressed with **were going to**, **could**, or **would**. The speaker wants the situation to be the opposite of what it will be. **Could**, not **would**, is used when the speaker is making a wish with *I*, as in (d). *INCORRECT:* I wish I would go with you.
(e) It is raining. I wish it *would stop*.	**Wish + would** can be used when the speaker wants an action or event to change, as in (e). Note that it cannot be used for situations. *INCORRECT:* I wish you would know the answer.
(f) I wish you *would leave* now.	**Wish + would** can also be used to make a strong request, as in (f).

Appendix

Supplementary Grammar Charts

UNIT A: Basic Grammar Terminology

A-1 Subjects, Verbs, and Objects

(a) $\overset{\text{S}}{Birds}$ $\overset{\text{V}}{fly}$. (noun) (verb)	Almost all English sentences contain a subject (**S**) and a verb (**V**). The verb may or may not be followed by an object (**O**).
(b) The $\overset{\text{S}}{baby}$ $\overset{\text{V}}{cried}$. (noun) (verb)	VERBS: Verbs that are not followed by an object, as in (a) and (b), are called "intransitive verbs." Common intransitive verbs: *agree, arrive, come, cry, exist, go, happen, live, occur, rain, rise, sleep, stay*.
(c) The $\overset{\text{S}}{student}$ $\overset{\text{V}}{needs}$ a $\overset{\text{O}}{pen}$. (noun) (verb) (noun)	Verbs that are followed by an object, as in (c) and (d), are called "transitive verbs." Common transitive verbs: *build, cut, find, like, make, need, send, use, want*.
(d) My $\overset{\text{S}}{friend}$ $\overset{\text{V}}{enjoyed}$ the $\overset{\text{O}}{party}$. (noun) (verb) (noun)	Some verbs can be either intransitive or transitive. Intransitive: *A student studies.* Transitive: *A student studies books.*
	SUBJECTS AND OBJECTS: The subjects and objects of verbs are nouns (or pronouns). Examples of nouns: *person, place, thing, John, Asia, pen, information, appearance, amusement*.

A-2 Adjectives

(a) Ann is an *intelligent* student. (adjective) (noun) (b) The *hungry* child ate fruit. (adjective) (noun)	Adjectives describe nouns. In grammar, we say that adjectives modify nouns. The word *modify* means "change a little." Adjectives give a little different meaning to a noun: *intelligent student, lazy student, good student*. Examples of adjectives: *young, old, rich, beautiful, brown, French, modern*.
(c) I saw some *beautiful* pictures. INCORRECT: beautiful ~~s~~ pictures	An adjective is neither singular nor plural. A final **-s** is never added to an adjective.

A-3 Adverbs

(a) He walks *quickly*. (adverb)	Adverbs modify verbs. Often they answer the question "How?" In (a): *How does he walk?* Answer: *Quickly.*

(b) She opened the door *quietly*.
                     (adverb)
	Adverbs are often formed by adding **-ly** to an adjective.
	    Adjective: *quick*
	    Adverb: *quickly*

(c) I am *extremely happy*. (adverb) (adjective)	Adverbs are also used to modify adjectives, i.e., to give information about adjectives, as in (c).
(d) Ann will come *tomorrow*. (adverb)	Adverbs are also used to express time or frequency. Examples: *tomorrow, today, yesterday, soon, never, usually, always, yet.*
MIDSENTENCE ADVERBS: (e) Ann *always comes* on time. (f) Ann *is always* on time. (g) Ann *has always come* on time. (h) Does *she always come* on time?	Some adverbs may occur in the middle of a sentence. Midsentence adverbs have usual positions; they • come in front of simple present and simple past verbs (except **be**), as in (e); • follow **be** (simple present and simple past), as in (f); • come between a helping verb and a main verb, as in (g). In a question, a midsentence adverb comes directly after the subject, as in (h).

Common midsentence adverbs

ever	usually	generally	seldom	never	already
always	often	sometimes	rarely	not ever	finally
	frequently	occasionally	hardly ever		just
					probably

A-4 Prepositions and Prepositional Phrases

Common prepositions

about	at	beyond	into	since	up
above	before	by	like	through	upon
across	behind	despite	near	throughout	with
after	below	down	of	till	within
against	beneath	during	off	to	without
along	beside	for	on	toward(s)	
among	besides	from	out	under	
around	between	in	over	until	

(a)   **S**   **V**   **PREP** **O of PREP**
    The student studies *in* the *library*.
                              (noun)
	An important element of English sentences is the prepositional phrase. It consists of a preposition (**PREP**) and its object (**o**). The object of a preposition is a noun or pronoun.
	
	In (a): *in the library* is a prepositional phrase.

(b)   **S**   **V**   **O**   **PREP**   **O of PREP**
    We enjoyed the party *at* your *house*.
                              (noun)	

(c) We went *to the zoo* *in the afternoon*. (Place) (Time) (d) *In the afternoon,* we went to the zoo.	In (c): In most English sentences, "place" comes before "time." In (d): Sometimes a prepositional phrase comes at the beginning of a sentence.

A
be absent from
be accused of
be accustomed to
be acquainted with
be addicted to
be afraid of
 agree with
be angry at, with
be annoyed with, by
 apologize for
 apply to, for
 approve of
 argue with, about
 arrive in, at
be associated with
be aware of

B
 believe in
 blame for
be blessed with
be bored with, by

C
be capable of
 care about, for
be cluttered with
be committed to
 compare to, with
 complain about, of
be composed of
be concerned about
be connected to
 consist of
be content with
 contribute to
be convinced of
be coordinated with
 count (up)on
be covered with
be crowded with

D
 decide (up)on
be dedicated to
 depend (up)on
be devoted to
be disappointed in, with
be discriminated against
 distinguish from
be divorced from
be done with

 dream of, about
be dressed in

E
be engaged in, to
be envious of
be equipped with
 escape from
 excel in, at
be excited about
 excuse for
be exhausted from
be exposed to

F
be faithful to
be familiar with
 feel like
 fight for
be filled with
be finished with
be fond of
 forget about
 forgive for
be friendly to, with
be frightened of, by
be furnished with

G
be gone from
be grateful to, for
be guilty of

H
 hide from
 hope for

I
be innocent of
 insist (up)on
be interested in
 introduce to
be involved in

J
be jealous of

K
 keep from
be known for

L
be limited to
be located in
 look forward to

M
be made of, from
be married to

O
 object to
be opposed to

P
 participate in
be patient with
be pleased with
be polite to
 pray for
be prepared for
 prevent from
 prohibit from
be protected from
be proud of
 provide with

Q
be qualified for

R
 recover from
be related to
be relevant to
 rely (up)on
be remembered for
 rescue from
 respond to
be responsible for

S
be satisfied with
be scared of, by
 stare at
 stop from
 subscribe to
 substitute for
 succeed in

T
 take advantage of
 take care of
 talk about, of
be terrified of, by
 thank for
 think about, of
be tired of, from

U
be upset with
be used to

V
 vote for

W
be worried about

UNIT B: Questions

B-1 Forms of Yes / No and Information Questions

A **yes/no question** = a question that may be answered by yes or no

A: Does he live in Chicago?
B: Yes, he does. OR No, he doesn't.

An **information question** = a question that asks for information by using a question word

A: Where does he live?
B: In Chicago.

Question word order = (Question word) + helping verb + subject + main verb

Notice that the same subject-verb order is used in both yes/no and information questions.

(Question Word)	Helping Verb	Subject	Main Verb	(Rest of Sentence)	
(a)	Does	she	live	there?	If the verb is in the simple present, use **does** (with he, she, it) or **do** (with I, you, we, they) in the question. If the verb is simple past, use **did**.
(b) Where	does	she	live?		
(c)	Do	they	live	there?	
(d) Where	do	they	live?		Notice: The main verb in the question is in its simple form; there is no final **-s** or **-ed**.
(e)	Did	he	live	there?	
(f) Where	did	he	live?		
(g)	Is	he	living	there?	If the verb has an auxiliary (a helping verb), the same auxiliary is used in the question. There is no change in the form of the main verb.
(h) Where	is	he	living?		
(i)	Have	they	lived	there?	
(j) Where	have	they	lived?		
(k)	Can	Mary	live	there?	If the verb has more than one auxiliary, only the first auxiliary precedes the subject, as in (m) and (n).
(l) Where	can	Mary	live?		
(m)	Will	he	be living	there?	
(n) Where	will	he	be living?		
(o) Who	Ø	Ø	lives	there?	If the question word is the subject, usual question-word order is not used; **does**, **do**, and **did** are not used. The verb is in the same form in a question as it is in a statement.
(p) Who	can	Ø	come?		
					Statement: *Tom came.*
					Question: *Who came?*
(q)	Are	they	Ø	there?	Main verb **be** in the simple present (am, is, are) and simple past (was, were) precedes the subject. It has the same position as a helping verb.
(r) Where	are	they?	Ø		
(s)	Was	Jim	Ø	there?	
(t) Where	was	Jim?	Ø		

B-2 Question Words

		Question	Answer	
When	(a)	*When* did they arrive? *When* will you come?	Yesterday. Next Monday.	***When*** is used to ask questions about *time*.
Where	(b)	*Where* is she? *Where* can I find a pen?	At home. In that drawer.	***Where*** is used to ask questions about *place*.
Why	(c)	*Why* did he leave early? *Why* aren't you coming with us?	Because he's ill. I'm tired.	***Why*** is used to ask questions about *reason*.
How	(d)	*How* did you come to school? *How* does he drive?	By bus. Carefully.	***How*** generally asks about *manner*.
	(e)	*How much* money does it cost? *How many* people came?	Ten dollars. Fifteen.	***How*** is used with ***much*** and ***many***.
	(f)	*How old* are you? *How cold* is it? *How soon* can you get here? *How fast* were you driving?	Twelve. Ten below zero. In ten minutes. 50 miles an hour.	***How*** is also used with adjectives and adverbs.
	(g)	*How long* has he been here? *How often* do you write home? *How far* is it to Miami from here?	Two years. Every week. 500 miles.	***How long*** asks about *length of time*. ***How often*** asks about *frequency*. ***How far*** asks about *distance*.
Who	(h)	*Who* can answer that question? *Who* came to visit you?	I can. Jane and Eric.	***Who*** is used as the subject of a question. It refers to people.
	(i)	*Who* is coming to dinner tonight? *Who* wants to come with me?	Ann, Bob, and Al. We do.	***Who*** is usually followed by a singular verb even if the speaker is asking about more than one person.
Whom	(j)	*Who(m)* did you see? *Who(m)* are you visiting?	I saw George. My relatives.	***Whom*** is used as the object of a verb or preposition. In everyday spoken English, ***whom*** is rarely used; ***who*** is used instead. ***Whom*** is used only in formal questions.
	(k)	*Who(m)* should I talk *to*? *To whom* should I talk? (formal)	The secretary.	NOTE: ***Whom***, not ***who***, is used if preceded by a preposition.
Whose	(l)	*Whose* book did you borrow? *Whose* key is this? (*Whose* is this?)	David's. It's mine.	***Whose*** asks questions about *possession*.

	Question	Answer	
What	(m) *What* made you angry? *What* went wrong?	His rudeness. Everything.	**What** is used as the subject of a question. It refers to things.
	(n) *What* do you need? *What* did Alice buy?	I need a pencil. A book.	**What** is also used as an object.
	(o) *What* did he talk *about*? *About* **what** did he talk? (formal)	His vacation.	
	(p) *What kind of* soup is that? *What kind of* shoes did he buy?	It's bean soup. Sandals.	**What kind of** asks about the particular variety or type of something.
	(q) *What* did you *do* last night? *What* is Mary *doing*?	I studied. Reading a book.	**What** + *a form of* **do** is used to ask questions about activities.
	(r) *What countries* did you visit? *What time* did she come? *What color* is his hair?	Italy and Spain. Seven o'clock. Dark brown.	**What** may accompany a noun.
	(s) *What* is Ed *like*?	He's kind and friendly.	**What** + **be like** asks for a general description of qualities.
	(t) *What* is the weather *like*?	Hot and humid.	
	(u) *What* does Ed *look like*?	He's tall and has dark hair.	**What** + **look like** asks for a physical description.
	(v) *What* does her house *look like*?	It's a two-story,* red brick house.	
Which	(w) I have two pens. *Which pen* do you want? *Which one* do you want? *Which do* you want?	The blue one.	**Which** is used instead of **what** when a question concerns choosing from a definite, known quantity or group.
	(x) *Which book* should I buy?	That one.	
	(y) *Which countries* did he visit? *What countries* did he visit?	Peru and Chile.	In some cases, there is little difference in meaning between **which** and **what** when they accompany a noun, as in (y) and (z).
	(z) *Which class* are you in? *What class* are you in?	This class.	

*American English: *a two-story house.*
British English: *a two-storey house.*

B-3 Shortened *Yes / No* Questions

(a) *Going to bed now? = Are you going to bed now?* (b) *Finish your work? = Did you finish your work?* (c) *Want to go to the movie with us? = Do you want to go to the movie with us?*	Sometimes in spoken English, the auxiliary and the subject **you** are dropped from a *yes/no* question, as in (a), (b), and (c).

B-4 Negative Questions

(a) *Doesn't she live* in the dormitory? (b) *Does she not live* in the dormitory? (very formal)	In a *yes/no* question in which the verb is negative, usually a contraction (e.g., *does + not = doesn't*) is used, as in (a). Example (b) is very formal and is usually not used in everyday speech. Negative questions are used to indicate the speaker's idea (i.e., what she/he believes is or is not true) or attitude (e.g., surprise, shock, annoyance, anger).
(c) Bob returns to his dorm room after his nine o'clock class. Matt, his roommate, is there. Bob is surprised. Bob says, "*What are you doing here? Aren't you supposed to be in class now?*"	In (c): Bob believes that Matt is supposed to be in class now. *Expected answer:* **Yes**.
(d) Alice and Mary are at home. Mary is about to leave on a trip, and Alice is going to take her to the airport. Alice says, "*It's already two o'clock. We'd better leave for the airport. Doesn't your plane leave at three?*"	In (d): Alice believes that Mary's plane leaves at three. She is asking the negative question to make sure that her information is correct. *Expected answer:* **Yes**.
(e) The teacher is talking to Jim about a test he failed. The teacher is surprised that Jim failed the test because he usually does very well. The teacher says, "*What happened? Didn't you study?*"	In (e): The teacher believes that Jim did not study. *Expected answer:* **No**.
(f) Barb and Ron are riding in a car. Ron is driving. He comes to a corner where there is a stop sign, but he does not stop the car. Barb is shocked. Barb says, "*What's the matter with you? Didn't you see that stop sign?*"	In (f): Barb believes that Ron did not see the stop sign. *Expected answer:* **No**.

B-5 Tag Questions

(a) Jack *can* come, *can't* he? (b) Fred *can't* come, *can* he?	A tag question is a question added at the end of a sentence. Speakers use tag questions mainly to make sure their information is correct or to seek agreement.*

AFFIRMATIVE SENTENCE + NEGATIVE TAG →	AFFIRMATIVE ANSWER EXPECTED
Mary *is* here, *isn't* she?	Yes, she is.
You *like* tea, *don't* you?	Yes, I do.
They *have left*, *haven't* they?	Yes, they have.

NEGATIVE SENTENCE + AFFIRMATIVE TAG →	NEGATIVE ANSWER EXPECTED
Mary *isn't* here, *is* she?	No, she isn't.
You *don't* like tea, *do* you?	No, I don't.
They *haven't* left, *have* they?	No, they haven't.

(c) *This / That* is your book, isn't *it*? *These / Those* are yours, aren't *they*?	The tag pronoun for ***this / that = it***. The tag pronoun for ***these / those = they***.
(d) *There is* a meeting tonight, *isn't there*?	In sentences with ***there + be, there*** is used in the tag.
(e) *Everything* is OK, isn't *it*? (f) *Everyone* took the test, didn't *they*?	Personal pronouns are used to refer to indefinite pronouns. ***They*** is usually used in a tag to refer to ***everyone, everybody, someone, somebody, no one, nobody***.
(g) *Nothing is* wrong, *is* it? (h) *Nobody called* on the phone, *did* they? (i) You*'ve never been* there, *have* you?	Sentences with negative words take affirmative tags.
(j) *I am* supposed to be here, *am I not*? (k) *I am* supposed to be here, *aren't I*?	In (j): ***am I not?*** is formal English. In (k): ***aren't I?*** is common in spoken English.

*A tag question may be spoken:
(1) with a rising intonation if the speaker is truly seeking to ascertain that his/her information, idea, belief is correct (e.g., *Ann lives in an apartment, doesn't she?*); OR
(2) with a falling intonation if the speaker is expressing an idea with which she/he is almost certain the listener will agree (e.g., *It's a nice day today, isn't it?*).

Jim *could* use some help, *couldn't* he?

UNIT C: Contractions

C Contractions

IN SPEAKING: In everyday spoken English, certain forms of **be** and auxiliary verbs are usually contracted with pronouns, nouns, and question words.

IN WRITING: (1) In written English, contractions with pronouns are common in informal writing, but they're not generally acceptable in formal writing.

(2) Contractions with nouns and question words are, for the most part, rarely used in writing. A few of these contractions may be found in quoted dialogue in stories or in very informal writing, such as a chatty letter to a good friend, but most of them are rarely if ever written.

In the following, quotation marks indicate that the contraction is frequently spoken but rarely, if ever, written.

	With Pronouns	**With Nouns**	**With Question Words**
am	*I'm* reading a book.	Ø	*"What'm"* I supposed to do?
is	*She's* studying. *It's* going to rain.	My *"book's"* on the table. *Mary's* at home.	*Where's* Sally? *Who's* that man?
are	*You're* working hard. *They're* waiting for us.	My *"books're"* on the table. The *"teachers're"* at a meeting.	*"What're"* you doing? *"Where're"* they going?
has	*She's* been here for a year. *It's* been cold lately.	My *"book's"* been stolen! *Sally's* never met him.	*Where's* Sally been living? *What's* been going on?
have	*I've* finished my work. *They've* never met you.	The *"books've"* been sold. The *"students've"* finished the test.	*"Where've"* they been? *"How've"* you been?
had	*He'd* been waiting for us. *We'd* forgotten about it.	The *"books'd"* been sold. *"Mary'd"* never met him before.	*"Where'd"* you been before that? *"Who'd"* been there before you?
did	Ø	Ø	*"What'd"* you do last night? *"How'd"* you do on the test?
will	*I'll* come later. *She'll* help us.	The *"weather'll"* be nice tomorrow. *"John'll"* be coming soon.	*"Who'll"* be at the meeting? *"Where'll"* you be at ten?
would	*He'd* like to go there. *They'd* come if they could.	My *"friends'd"* come if they could. *"Mary'd"* like to go there too.	*"Where'd"* you like to go?

UNIT D: Negatives

D-1 Using *Not* and Other Negative Words

(a) AFFIRMATIVE: The earth is round. (b) NEGATIVE: The earth is *not* flat.	*Not* expresses a *negative* idea.

	AUX	+ *NOT* +	MAIN VERB		*Not* immediately follows an auxiliary verb or *be*.
(c) I	will	not	go	there.	NOTE: If there is more than one auxiliary, *not* comes immediately after the first auxiliary: *I will not be* going there.
I	have	not	gone	there.	*Do* or *does* is used with *not* to make a simple present verb (except *be*) negative.
I	am	not	going	there.	*Did* is used with *not* to make a simple past verb (except *be*) negative.
I	was	not		there.	
I	do	not	go	there.	
He	does	not	go	there.	
I	did	not	go	there.	

Contractions of auxiliary verbs with *not*

are not = aren't* cannot = can't could not = couldn't did not = didn't does not = doesn't do not = don't	has not = hasn't have not = haven't had not = hadn't is not = isn't must not = mustn't should not = shouldn't	was not = wasn't were not = weren't will not = won't would not = wouldn't

(d) I almost *never* go there. I have *hardly ever* gone there.	In addition to *not*, the following are negative adverbs: *never, rarely, seldom* *hardly (ever), scarcely (ever), barely (ever)*
(e) There's *no* chalk in the drawer.	*No* also expresses a negative idea.
COMPARE: *NOT* VS. *NO* (f) I *do not have* any money. (g) I have *no money*.	*Not* is used to make a verb negative, as in (f). *No* is used as an adjective in front of a noun (e.g., money), as in (g). NOTE: Examples (f) and (g) have the same meaning.

*Sometimes in spoken English you will hear "ain't." It means "am not," "isn't," or "aren't." *Ain't* is not considered proper English although it is frequently used for humor.

D-2 Avoiding Double Negatives

(a) INCORRECT: I ~~don't~~ have ~~no~~ money. (b) CORRECT: I *don't* have *any* money. CORRECT: I have *no* money.	Sentence (a) is an example of a "double negative," i.e., a confusing and grammatically incorrect sentence that contains two negatives in the same clause. One clause should contain only one negative.*

*Negatives in two different clauses in the same sentence cause no problems; for example:
   *A person who **doesn't** have love **can't** be truly happy.*
   *I **don't** know why he **isn't** here.*

D-3 Beginning a Sentence with a Negative Word

(a) *Never will I do* that again! (b) *Rarely have I eaten* better food. (c) *Hardly ever does he come* to class on time.	When a negative word begins a sentence, the subject and verb are inverted (i.e., question word order is used).*

*Beginning a sentence with a negative word is relatively uncommon in everyday usage; it is used when the speaker/writer wishes to emphasize the negative element of the sentence and be expressive.

UNIT E: Verbs

E-1 The Verb *Be*

(a)	John	*is*	*a student*.
		(*be*)	(noun)
(b)	John	*is*	*intelligent*.
		(*be*)	(adjective)
(c)	John	*was*	*at the library*.
		(*be*)	(prep. phrase)

A sentence with *be* as the main verb has three basic patterns:

In (a): *be* + *a noun*
In (b): *be* + *an adjective*
In (c): *be* + *a prepositional phrase*

(d)	Mary *is writing* a letter.
(e)	They *were listening* to some music.
(f)	That letter *was written* by Alice.

Be is also used as an auxiliary verb in progressive verb tenses and in the passive.

In (d): *is* = auxiliary; *writing* = main verb

Tense Forms of *Be*

	SIMPLE PRESENT	SIMPLE PAST	PRESENT PERFECT
SINGULAR	*I am* *you are* *he, she, it is*	*I was* *you were* *he, she, it was*	*I have been* *you have been* *he, she, it has been*
PLURAL	*we, you, they are*	*we, you, they were*	*we, you, they have been*

E-2 Spelling of *-ing* and *-ed* Verb Forms

(1)	VERBS THAT END IN A CONSONANT AND *-e*	(a)	hope date injure	hoping dating injuring	hoped dated injured	*-ING* FORM: If the word ends in *-e*, drop the *-e* and add *-ing*.* *-ED* FORM: If the word ends in a consonant and *-e*, just add *-d*.

(2)	VERBS THAT END IN A VOWEL AND A CONSONANT	ONE-SYLLABLE VERBS			
		(b)	stop rob	stopping robbing	stopped robbed	1 vowel → 2 consonants**
		(c)	rain fool	raining fooling	rained fooled	2 vowels → 1 consonant
		TWO-SYLLABLE VERBS			
		(d)	listen offer	listening offering	listened offered	1st syllable stressed → 1 consonant
		(e)	begin prefer	beginning preferring	(began) preferred	2nd syllable stressed → 2 consonants

(3)	VERBS THAT END IN TWO CONSONANTS	(f)	start fold demand	starting folding demanding	started folded demanded	If the word ends in two consonants, just add the ending.

(4)	VERBS THAT END IN *-y*	(g)	enjoy pray	enjoying praying	enjoyed prayed	If *-y* is preceded by a vowel, keep the *-y*.
		(h)	study try reply	studying trying replying	studied tried replied	If *-y* is preceded by a consonant: *-ING* FORM: keep the *-y*; add *-ing*. *-ED* FORM: change *-y* to *-i*; add *-ed*.

(5)	VERBS THAT END IN *-ie*	(i)	die lie	dying lying	died lied	*-ING* FORM: Change *-ie* to *-y*; add *-ing*. *-ED* FORM: Change *-y* to *-i*; add *-ed*.

*Exception: If a verb ends in *-ee*, the final *-e* is not dropped: *seeing, agreeing, freeing*.

**Exception: *-w* and *-x* are not doubled: *plow* → *plowed; fix* → *fixed*.

The Simple Tenses

This basic diagram will be used in all tense descriptions.

SIMPLE PRESENT	(a) It *snows* in Alaska. (b) Tom *watches* TV every day.	In general, the simple present expresses events or situations that exist *always, usually, habitually;* they exist now, have existed in the past, and probably will exist in the future.
SIMPLE PAST	(c) It *snowed* yesterday. (d) Tom *watched* TV last night.	*At one particular time in the past,* this happened. It began and ended in the past.
SIMPLE FUTURE	(e) It *will snow* tomorrow. It *is going to snow* tomorrow. (f) Tom *will watch* TV tonight. Tom *is going to watch* TV tonight.	*At one particular time in the future,* this will happen.

The Progressive Tenses

Form: *be* + *-ing* (*present participle*)

Meaning: The progressive tenses* give the idea that an action is in progress during a particular time. The tenses say that an action *begins before, is in progress during, and continues after* another time or action.

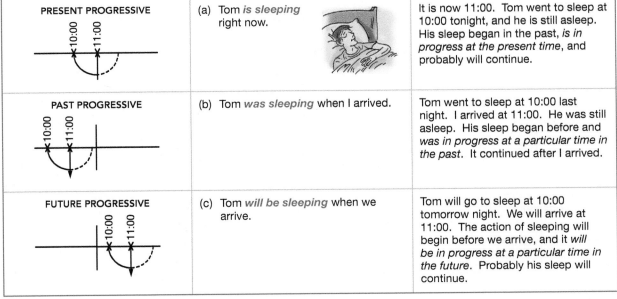

PRESENT PROGRESSIVE	(a) Tom *is sleeping* right now.	It is now 11:00. Tom went to sleep at 10:00 tonight, and he is still asleep. His sleep began in the past, *is in progress at the present time,* and probably will continue.
PAST PROGRESSIVE	(b) Tom *was sleeping* when I arrived.	Tom went to sleep at 10:00 last night. I arrived at 11:00. He was still asleep. His sleep began before and *was in progress at a particular time in the past.* It continued after I arrived.
FUTURE PROGRESSIVE	(c) Tom *will be sleeping* when we arrive.	Tom will go to sleep at 10:00 tomorrow night. We will arrive at 11:00. The action of sleeping will begin before we arrive, and it *will be in progress at a particular time in the future.* Probably his sleep will continue.

*The progressive tenses are also called the "continuous" tenses: present continuous, past continuous, and future continuous.

(continued)

The Perfect Tenses

Form: *have* + *past participle*

Meaning: The perfect tenses all give the idea that one thing *happens before* another time or event.

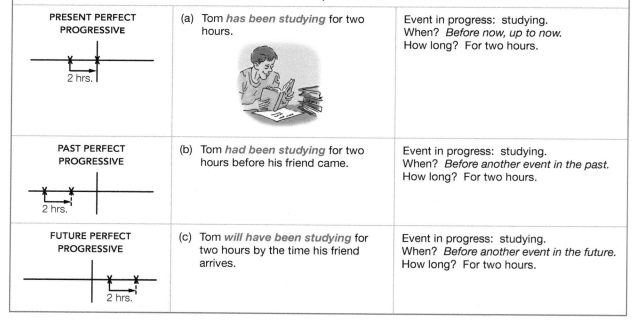

PRESENT PERFECT	(a) Tom *has* already *eaten*.	Tom *finished* eating *sometime before now*. The exact time is not important.
PAST PERFECT	(b) Tom *had* already *eaten* when his friend arrived.	First Tom finished eating. Later his friend arrived. Tom's eating was completely *finished before another time in the past*.
FUTURE PERFECT	(c) Tom *will* already *have eaten* when his friend arrives.	First Tom will finish eating. Later his friend will arrive. Tom's eating will be completely *finished before another time in the future*.

The Perfect Progressive Tenses

Form: *have* + *been* + *-ing (present participle)*

Meaning: The perfect progressive tenses give the idea that one event is *in progress immediately before, up to, until another time or event*. The tenses are used to express the duration of the first event.

PRESENT PERFECT PROGRESSIVE	(a) Tom *has been studying* for two hours.	Event in progress: studying. When? *Before now, up to now.* How long? For two hours.
PAST PERFECT PROGRESSIVE	(b) Tom *had been studying* for two hours before his friend came.	Event in progress: studying. When? *Before another event in the past.* How long? For two hours.
FUTURE PERFECT PROGRESSIVE	(c) Tom *will have been studying* for two hours by the time his friend arrives.	Event in progress: studying. When? *Before another event in the future.* How long? For two hours.

Simple Present

Tom *studies* every day.

Present Progressive

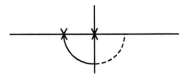

Tom *is studying* right now.

Simple Past

Tom *studied* last night.

Past Progressive

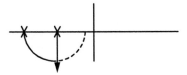

Tom *was studying* when they came.

Simple Future

Tom *will study* tomorrow.
Tom *is going to study* tomorrow.

Future Progressive

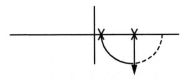

Tom *will be studying* when they come.
Tom *is going to be studying* when they come.

Present Perfect

Tom *has* already *studied* Chapter 1.

Present Perfect Progressive

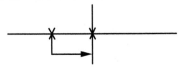

Tom *has been studying* for two hours.

Past Perfect

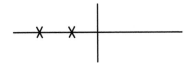

Tom *had* already *studied* Chapter 1 before he began studying Chapter 2.

Past Perfect Progressive

Tom *had been studying* for two hours before his friends came.

Future Perfect

Tom *will* already *have studied* Chapter 4 before he studies Chapter 5.

Future Perfect Progressive

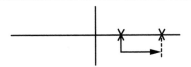

Tom *will have been studying* for two hours by the time his roommate gets home.

E-5 Regular Verbs: Pronunciation of -ed Endings

Final **-ed** has three different pronunciations: /t/, /d/, and /əd/. The schwa /ə/ is an unstressed vowel sound. It is pronounced like *a* in *alone* in normal, rapid speech (e.g., *She lives alone.*).

(a) looked → look/t/ clapped → clap/t/ missed → miss/t/ watched → watch/t/ finished → finish/t/ laughed → laugh/t/	Final **-ed** is pronounced /t/ after voiceless sounds. Voiceless sounds are made by pushing air through your mouth; no sound comes from your throat. Examples of voiceless sounds: "k," "p," "s," "ch," "sh," "f."
(b) smelled → smell/d/ saved → save/d/ cleaned → clean/d/ robbed → rob/d/ played → play/d/	Final **-ed** is pronounced /d/ after voiced sounds. Voiced sounds come from your throat. If you touch your neck when you make a voiced sound, you can feel your voice box vibrate. Examples of voiced sounds: "l," "v," "n," "b," and all vowel sounds.
(c) decided → decide/əd/ needed → need/əd/ wanted → want/əd/ invited → invite/əd/	Final **-ed** is pronounced /əd/ after "t" and "d" sounds. The sound /əd/ adds a whole syllable to a word. COMPARE: looked = one syllable → look/t/ smelled = one syllable → smell/d/ needed = two syllables → need/əd/

E-6 Pronunciation of Final -s in Verbs and Nouns

Final **-s** has three different pronunciations: /s/, /z/, and /əz/.

(a) seats → *seat*/s/ ropes → *rope*/s/ backs → *back*/s/	Final **-s** is pronounced /s/ after voiceless sounds, as in (a). "t," "p," and "k" are examples of voiceless sounds.
(b) seeds → *seed*/z/ robes → *robe*/z/ bags → *bag*/z/ sees → *see*/z/	Final **-s** is pronounced /z/ after voiced sounds, as in (b). "d," "b," "g," and "ee" are examples of voiced sounds.
(c) dishes → *dish*/əz/ catches → *catch*/əz/ kisses → *kiss*/əz/ mixes → *mix*/əz/ prizes → *prize*/əz/ edges → *edge*/əz/	Final **-s** and **-es** are pronounced /əz/ after "sh," "ch," "s," "x," "z," and "ge"/"dge" sounds. The /əz/ ending adds a syllable. All of the words in (c) are pronounced with two syllables. COMPARE: All of the words in (a) and (b) are pronounced with one syllable.

E-7 Linking Verbs

(a) The soup *smells* *good*. (linking verb) (adjective) (b) This food *tastes delicious*. (c) The children *feel happy*. (d) The weather *became cold*.	Other verbs like *be* that may be followed immediately by an adjective are called "linking verbs." An adjective following a linking verb describes the subject of a sentence.* Common verbs that may be followed by an adjective: • *feel, look, smell, sound, taste* • *appear, seem* • *become* (and *get, turn, grow* when they mean "become")

*COMPARE:

    (1) *The man looks angry.* → An adjective (***angry***) follows ***look***. The adjective describes the subject (***the man***). ***Look*** has the meaning of "appear."

    (2) *The man looked at me angrily.* → An adverb (***angrily***) follows l***ook at***. The adverb describes the action of the verb. ***Look at*** has the meaning of "regard, watch."

Ann *is* **at the laudromat**.
She **looks** very **busy**.

E-8 Troublesome Verbs: *Raise / Rise, Set / Sit, Lay / Lie*

Transitive	Intransitive	
		Raise, ***set***, and ***lay*** are *transitive* verbs; they are followed by an object. ***Rise***, ***sit***, and ***lie*** are intransitive; they are NOT followed by an object.*
(a) *raise, raised, raised* Tom ***raised*** his hand.	(b) *rise, rose, risen* The sun ***rises*** in the east.	
(c) *set, set, set* I ***will set*** the book on the desk.	(d) *sit, sat, sat* I ***sit*** in the front row.	In (a): ***raised*** is followed by the object ***hand***. In (b): ***rises*** is not followed by an object.

(e) *lay, laid, laid*
I ***am laying*** the book on the desk.
	(f) *lie,** lay, lain*
	He *is **lying*** on his bed.
		NOTE: ***Lay*** and ***lie*** are troublesome for native speakers too and are frequently misused.
		     lay = put
		     lie = recline

   *See Appendix Chart A-1 for information about transitive and intransitive verbs.

  Lie* is a regular verb (*lie, lied*) when it means "not tell the truth": ***He lied to me about his age.*

E-9 Irregular Verbs: An Alphabetical Reference List

NOTE: Verbs followed by a bullet (•) are defined at the end of the this list.

Simple Form	Simple Past	Past Participle	Simple Form	Simple Past	Past Participle
arise	arose	arisen	forbid	forbade	forbidden
awake	awoke	awoken	forecast•	forecast	forecast
be	was, were	been	forget	forgot	forgotten
bear	bore	borne/born	forgive	forgave	forgiven
beat	beat	beaten/beat	forsake•	forsook	forsaken
become	became	become	freeze	froze	frozen
begin	began	begun	get	got	gotten/got*
bend	bent	bent	give	gave	given
bet•	bet	bet	go	went	gone
bid•	bid	bid	grind•	ground	ground
bind•	bound	bound	grow	grew	grown
bite	bit	bitten	hang**	hung	hung
bleed	bled	bled	have	had	had
blow	blew	blown	hear	heard	heard
break	broke	broken	hide	hid	hidden
breed•	bred	bred	hit	hit	hit
bring	brought	brought	hold	held	held
broadcast•	broadcast	broadcast	hurt	hurt	hurt
build	built	built	keep	kept	kept
burn	burned/burnt	burned/burnt	kneel	kneeled/knelt	kneeled/knelt
burst•	burst	burst	know	knew	known
buy	bought	bought	lay	laid	laid
cast•	cast	cast	lead	led	led
catch	caught	caught	lean	leaned/leant	leaned/leant
choose	chose	chosen	leap	leaped/leapt	leaped/leapt
cling•	clung	clung	learn	learned/learnt	learned/learnt
come	came	come	leave	left	left
cost	cost	cost	lend	lent	lent
creep•	crept	crept	let	let	let
cut	cut	cut	lie	lay	lain
deal•	dealt	dealt	light	lighted/lit	lighted/lit
dig	dug	dug	lose	lost	lost
do	did	done	make	made	made
draw	drew	drawn	mean	meant	meant
dream	dreamed/dreamt	dreamed/dreamt	meet	met	met
drink	drank	drunk	mislay	mislaid	mislaid
drive	drove	driven	mistake	mistook	mistaken
eat	ate	eaten	pay	paid	paid
fall	fell	fallen	prove	proved	proven/proved
feed	fed	fed	put	put	put
feel	felt	felt	quit***	quit	quit
fight	fought	fought	read	read	read
find	found	found	rid	rid	rid
fit	fit/fitted	fit/fitted	ride	rode	ridden
flee•	fled	fled	ring	rang	rung
fling•	flung	flung	rise	rose	risen
fly	flew	flown			

*In British English: *get–got–got.* In American English: *get–got–gotten/got.*

****Hang* is a regular verb when it means to kill someone with a rope around his/her neck.

COMPARE: **I hung** my clothes in the closet. They **hanged** the murderer by the neck until he was dead.

***Also possible in British English: *quit–quitted–quitted.*

Simple Form	Simple Past	Past Participle	Simple Form	Simple Past	Past Participle
run	ran	run	spring•	sprang/sprung	sprung
say	said	said	stand	stood	stood
see	saw	seen	steal	stole	stolen
seek•	sought	sought	stick	stuck	stuck
sell	sold	sold	sting•	stung	stung
send	sent	sent	stink•	stank/stunk	stunk
set	set	set	strike•	struck	struck/stricken
shake	shook	shaken	strive•	strove/strived	striven/strived
shed•	shed	shed	string	strung	strung
shine	shone/shined	shone/shined	swear	swore	sworn
shoot	shot	shot	sweep	swept	swept
show	showed	shown/showed	swell	swelled	swelled/swollen
shrink•	shrank/shrunk	shrunk	swim	swam	swum
shut	shut	shut	swing•	swung	swung
sing	sang	sung	take	took	taken
sink•	sank	sunk	teach	taught	taught
sit	sat	sat	tear	tore	torn
sleep	slept	slept	tell	told	told
slide•	slid	slid	think	thought	thought
slit•	slit	slit	throw	threw	thrown
smell	smelled/smelt	smelled/smelt	thrust•	thrust	thrust
sneak	sneaked/snuck	sneaked/snuck	understand	understood	understood
speak	spoke	spoken	undertake	undertook	undertaken
speed	sped/speeded	sped/speeded	upset	upset	upset
spell	spelled/spelt	spelled/spelt	wake	woke/waked	woken
spend	spent	spent	wear	wore	worn
spill	spilled/spilt	spilled/spilt	weave•	wove	woven
spin•	spun	spun	weep•	wept	wept
spit	spit/spat	spit/spat	win	won	won
split•	split	split	wind•	wound	wound
spoil	spoiled/spoilt	spoiled/spoilt	withdraw	withdrew	withdrawn
spread•	spread	spread	write	wrote	written

•Definitions of some of the less frequently used irregular verbs:

bet . . . . . wager; offer to pay money if one loses

bid . . . . . make an offer of money, usually at a public sale

bind . . . . . fasten or secure

breed . . . . . bring animals together to produce young

broadcast . . . . . send information by radio waves; announce

burst . . . . . explode; break suddenly

cast . . . . . throw

cling . . . . . hold on tightly

creep . . . . . crawl close to the ground; move slowly and quietly

deal . . . . . distribute playing cards to each person; give attention to (deal with)

flee . . . . . escape; run away

fling . . . . . throw with force

forecast . . . . . predict a future occurrence

forsake . . . . . abandon or desert

grind . . . . . crush, reduce to small pieces

seek . . . . . look for

shed . . . . . drop off or get rid of

shrink . . . . . become smaller

sink . . . . . move downward, often under water

slide . . . . . glide smoothly; slip or skid

slit . . . . . cut a narrow opening

spin . . . . . turn rapidly around a central point

split . . . . . divide into two or more parts

spread . . . . . push out in all directions (e.g., butter on bread, news)

spring . . . . . jump or rise suddenly from a still position

sting . . . . . cause pain with a sharp object (e.g., pin) or bite (e.g., by an insect)

stink . . . . . have a bad or foul smell

strike . . . . . hit something with force

strive . . . . . try hard to achieve a goal

swing . . . . . move back and forth

thrust . . . . . push forcibly; shove

weave . . . . . form by passing pieces of material over and under each other (as in making baskets, cloth)

weep . . . . . cry

wind . . . . . (sounds like *find*) turn around and around

Index

Able to, 44, 48, 52 (*Look on pages 44, 48, and 52.*)	The numbers following the words listed in the index refer to page numbers in the text.
Continuous tenses, 119*fn.* (*Look at the footnote on page 119.*)	The letters *fn.* mean "footnote." Footnotes appear beneath some charts.

A

A/an, 29, 33, 34, 36, 36*fn.*
Able to, 44, 48, 52
Accustomed to, 78
A couple of, 31
Active verbs, 58
Adjective(s), 108
    after *being* (e.g., *being foolish*), 3*fn.*
    defined, 108
    after *get* (e.g., *get hungry*), 61
    infinitives after (e.g., *happy to meet*), 83
    with linking verbs (e.g., *taste good*), 123
    non-progressive passive verbs used as, 60
    nouns used as (e.g., *vegetable soup*), 28
    participial (e.g., *amusing/amused*), 62
    possessive (*my, your,* etc.), 39, 40, 87
    preposition combinations with, 110
    used as nouns (e.g., *the poor*), 25, 29
Adjective clauses:
    defined, 69
    expressions of quantity in, 73
    object pronouns in (*whom, which, that*), 70
    prepositions in, 70, 71
    pronouns modified by, 72
    punctuation of, 73
    reducing to modifying phrases, 74
    subject pronouns in (*who, which, that*), 69, 74
    with *when,* 71
    with *where,* 71
    with *which,* 69, 69*fn.,* 70, 72*fn.,* 74
    with *whose,* 71
Adjective phrases, 74, 74*fn.*

Adverb(s), 109
    conjunctive (e.g., *therefore*), 99
    defined, 109
    list of, 109
    midsentence, 109
    with past perfect, 15
    with present perfect, 11
Adverb clauses, 90
    of cause and effect (*because,* etc.), 90, 92, 97, 98
    of condition (*if, unless,* etc.), 90, 93, 94, 98, 103
    as connectives, 98, 100
    of contrast (*although,* etc.), 90, 92, 98, 102
    defined, 90
    of direct contrast (*whereas, while*), 90, 92, 102
    punctuation of, 90, 100
    of purpose (*so that*), 101
    reducing to modifying phrases, 95–97
    of time (*after, before,* etc.), 19, 90, 91
    words used to introduce, 90
Advise, 76*fn.*
A few, 31
Affirmatives, in tag questions, 115
Afraid, 65*fn.*
After, 15, 91, 91*fn.,* 96
A great deal of, 31, 32
Agreement:
    with paired conjunctions, 89
    pronoun with noun, 40
    subject-verb, 23, 24, 25
Ain't, 117*fn.*

A little, 31
All (of), 31, 32, 32*fn.*
All day/morning/week, 14
A lot of, 29, 31, 32
Although, 92*fn.,* 98, 102
Am/is/are being + adjective, 3*fn.*
Am/is/are going to, 17
And, 23, 88, 89
And, but, or, nor, 88
Another, 42, 43
Antecedent, 39
A number of, 24, 31
Any, 31
Apostrophes:
    in contractions, 116–117
    with possessive nouns, 28, 29
    with possessive pronouns, 39
Appositives, 74
Articles:
    with definite and indefinite nouns, 33
    with generic nouns, 34
    guidelines for using, 36
As, 91
A/some, 33
As/so long as, 91
As soon as, 91
Auxiliary verbs (SEE *Be;* Contractions of verbs;
    Do/does/did; Have/has/had; Modal
    auxiliaries; Questions)

B

Be, 118
    with modal + *-ing,* 54
    in passive form, 58
Be able to, 44, 48, 55, 57
Be accustomed to, 78
Because:
    in adverb clauses, 90, 92, 98
    in adverbial phrases, 97
    vs. *even though,* 92
Because of, 99
Before, 15, 91, 91*fn.,* 96
Be going to:
    in conditional sentences, 104
    after modals, 55
    summary chart of, 56
    tense forms of, 3, 17, 20
    vs. *will,* 18
Being + adjective, 3*fn.*
Be supposed to, 47, 56

Be used for, 83*fn.*
Be used to, 83*fn.*
Both ... and, 89
But, 88, 89, 98, 102
    vs. *though,* 102*fn.*
By:
    in passive form (the *by*-phrase), 58, 59, 60
    with reflexive pronouns, 41
By the time, 15, 91

C

Can, 44
    in conditional sentences, 104
    degree of certainty in, 52, 53
    in expressions of ability, 48
    in expressions of permission, 49
    in expressions of possibility, 48
    in polite requests, 49
    after *so that,* 101
    summary chart of, 57
Causative verbs (*make, have, get*), 87
Clauses, defined, 63, 69, 74 (SEE ALSO Adjective
    clauses; Adverb clauses; Dependent
    clauses; Independent clauses; Noun
    clauses; Time clauses)
Collective nouns, 23, 40
Commands (SEE Imperative sentences)
Commas:
    with adjective clauses, 73, 73*fn.,* 100
    with adjective phrases, 74
    with adverb clauses, 90, 100
    with conjunctions, 100
    with independent clauses, 89
    inverted, 66*fn.*
    in parallel structures, 88, 88*fn.*
    with prepositions, 100
    in quoted speech, 66
    with transitions, 99
    with *while*-clauses, 102*fn.*
Complex sentences (SEE Adjective clauses;
    Adverb clauses; Noun clauses)
Conditional sentences:
    basic verb forms used in, 104
    expressions of real conditions in, 104
    expressions of unreal conditions in,
        104, 105
    implied conditions in, 107
    mixed time in, 106
    omission of *if* in, 106, 107
    progressive verb forms used in, 106

Conjunctions:
    as connectives, 98, 100
    coordinating, 88, 89
    in expressions of cause and effect, 98, 99
    in expressions of condition, 98, 103
    in expressions of contrast, 98, 102
    independent clauses connected with, 89
    paired (correlative), 89, 89*fn.*
    punctuation with, 88, 89, 100
    subordinating, 90*fn.*
Conjunctive adverbs, 99 (SEE ALSO Transitions)
Consequently, 98, 99
Continuous tenses, 119*fn.*
Contractions of verbs, 116–117
    with *not,* 117
    with nouns, 17, 116
    with personal names, 12
    with pronouns, 11, 15, 17, 116
Contrary to fact (SEE Conditional sentences)
Coordinating conjunctions, 88, 89
Correlative (paired) conjunctions, 89, 89*fn.*
Could, 44
    in conditional sentences, 105
    degree of certainty in, 52, 53, 54
    in expressions of past ability, 52
    in polite requests, 49
    in reported speech, 68
    after *so that,* 101
    in suggestions/advice, 46
    summary chart of, 57
    after *wish,* 107
Count/noncount nouns:
    defined, 29
    expressions of quantity with, 30*fn.,* 31
    list of, 30

D

Dangling modifiers, 95
Definite nouns, 33, 34
Dependent clauses, defined, 63, 90 (SEE ALSO
    Adjective clauses; Adverb clauses; Noun
    clauses)
Despite, 102
Direct speech, 66*fn.* (SEE ALSO Quoted speech)
Do/does/did:
    contractions with, 116
    in negatives, 117
    in questions, 111

Double negatives, 117
Due to, 99

E

Each/every, 23, 31, 32, 32*fn.*
Each of, 24, 32
-Ed forms, 4, 7
    in participial adjectives, 62
    pronunciation of, 122
    spelling of, 118
Either … or, 89
-En forms, 8
Enough, 84
Even if, 93, 98
Even though, 92, 92*fn.,* 98, 102
Everyone, 32*fn.*
Every one (of), 24, 32
    vs. *everyone,* 32*fn.*
Every time, 91
Except, 43
Exclamation points, 66
Expressions:
    of ability, 48, 52
    of advisability, 46, 51
    of cause and effect, 98, 99, 100
    of condition, 98, 103
    of contrast, 98, 102
    of degree of certainty, 52, 53, 54
    of expectation, 47, 51
    of necessity, 45, 51
    with *other,* 43
    of permission, 49, 50
    of place, 24, 24*fn.*
    of possibility, 48
    of preference, 55
    of purpose, 83, 101
    of quantity, 23, 30*fn.,* 31, 32, 73
    of real conditions, 104
    special, followed by *-ing* (e.g., *have fun doing*), 79
    of suggestions, 46, 50
    of unreal conditions, 104, 105

F

(A) Few/(a) little, 31
For:
    in expressions of purpose, 83
    vs. *since,* 10, 14
Forget/remember, 77, 77*fn.*
Frequency adverbs, 109

Full stop, 89*fn*. (SEE ALSO Periods)
Future time:
    making wishes in, 107
    present tenses to express, 19
    time clauses to express, 19
    (SEE ALSO **Be going to;** Verb tenses; **Will**)

G

Generic nouns, 34, 40
Gerunds:
    after *advise,* 76*fn*.
    common verbs followed by, 75, 77, 81
    defined, 75
    after *go,* 78
    after *need,* 85
    as objects of prepositions, 78, 82
    passive, 84, 85
    past forms of, 85
    possessive adjectives and nouns modifying, 87
    as subjects, 23, 79
Get:
    as causative verb (e.g., *get them to do it*), 87
    passive with (e.g., *get worried*), 61
Go + gerund (e.g., *go shopping*), 78
Going to, 17, 20
    vs. *will,* 18
Got to, 45

H

Habitual past, 51
Had better, 44, 46, 51, 56
Had to, 51, 68
Have got to, 45, 51, 56
Have/has/had:
    as causative verb, 87
    in conditional sentences, 106
    contractions with, 11, 15, 116
    as helping vs. main verb, 71*fn*.
    in past infinitives and gerunds, 85
    in present perfect, 10, 11
    in reduced speech, 12, 16
Have to:
    in expressions of necessity, 45
    after modals, 55
    summary chart of, 56
Help, 86
Hope, 6, 107
How, 112
However, 98, 102
How long, 14, 112
Hyphen, 28

I

-Ics words, 25
If:
    in adverb clauses of condition, 93, 98, 103
    in noun clauses, 64
    (SEE ALSO Conditional sentences; Noun
        clauses)
***If*-**clauses, 93, 104
    implied, 107
If ... not, 94
Imperative sentences, 67
Impersonal pronouns, 41
In case, 94, 98
Indefinite nouns, 33, 34
Indefinite pronouns, 40, 72
Independent clauses, defined, 63, 89
Indirect speech, 66*fn*. (SEE ALSO Reported
    speech)
Infinitives:
    after adjectives, 83
    after *be,* 47
    common verbs followed by, 76, 77, 80
    defined, 75
    with *get* as causative verb, 87
    with *it,* 79
    with modal auxiliaries, 44
    after *need,* 85
    with objects, 76
    passive, 84, 85
    past forms of, 85
    of purpose (*in order to*), 83, 83*fn*.
    after question words, 65
    as subjects, 79
    with *too/enough,* 84
Information questions, 111
-Ing forms:
    in adverbial phrases, 95, 97
    go + *-ing,* 78
    modal + *be* + *-ing,* 54
    in participial adjectives, 62
    special expressions followed by (e.g., *have fun*
        doing), 79
    spelling of, 118
    upon + *-ing,* 97
    after verbs of perception (e.g., *see her walking*), 86
    (SEE ALSO Gerunds; Present participles)
In order that, 101*fn*.
In order to, 83, 83*fn*., 101
In spite of, 102
Intend, 6, 76*fn*.
Intransitive verbs, 58, 123
Inverted commas, 66*fn*.

Inverted word order:
    after negatives, 117
    after *only if*, 94
In which, 71
Irregular plural nouns, 27
Irregular verbs, 4
    list of, 8–9, 124–125
It:
    agreement with, 40
    with infinitives, 79
    its vs. *it's*, 38
    in noun clauses, 65

J

Just:
    with present perfect, 11

K

Know how to, 48

L

Lay/lie, 123
Let, 86
Let's, 50
Linking verbs, 123
(A) Little/(a) few, 31
Lots of, 31, 32
-Ly, in adverbs, 109

M

Main clauses (SEE Independent clauses)
Make, as causative verb (e.g., *make them do it*), 87
Many/much, 29, 32
Many of, 32
May, 44
    degree of certainty in, 52, 53, 54
    in expressions of permission, 49
    in expressions of possibility, 48
    in polite requests, 49
    in reported speech, 68
    after *so that*, 101*fn*.
    summary chart of, 56
Maybe:
    degree of certainty in, 52
    vs. *may be*, 52
    in suggestions/advice, 46
Midsentence adverbs, 109
Might, 44
    in conditional sentences, 104
    degree of certainty in, 52, 53, 54

in expressions of possibility, 48
    in polite requests, 49*fn*.
    in reported speech, 68
    after *so that*, 101*fn*.
    in suggestions/advice, 46*fn*.
    summary chart of, 56
Modal auxiliaries:
    in conditional sentences, 104
    defined, 44
    list of, 44
    passive form of, 59
    phrasal modals after, 55
    in polite requests, 49
    progressive forms of, 54
    in reported speech, 68
    summary chart of, 56–57
Modify, defined, 108
Modifying phrases:
    reducing adjective phrases to, 74
    reducing adverb clauses to, 95–97
Most (of), 24, 31, 32
Much/many, 29, 31
Must, 44
    degree of certainty in, 52, 53
    in expressions of necessity, 45, 51
    in prohibitions, 45
    summary chart of, 56

N

Need:
    in expressions of necessity, 45*fn*.
    gerunds and infinitives after, 85
Negative questions, 114
Negative words, 117
Negatives, double, 117
Neither … nor, 89
Nevertheless/nonetheless, 98
No, 31, 117
Noncount nouns:
    defined, 29
    expressions of quantity with, 30*fn*., 31
    list of, 30
None (of), 24, 32
Non-progressive (stative) verbs:
    defined, 3
    passive, 60
    prepositions after, 60
Nonrestrictive adjective clauses, 73*fn*.
Nor, 88
Not, 117
Not only … but also, 89

Noun(s):
    collective, 23, 40
    contractions with, 17, 116
    count and noncount, 29, 30, 31
    defined, 108
    definite and indefinite, 33, 34
    generic, 34, 40
    possessive, 28, 29, 87
    pronoun agreement with, 40
    regular and irregular plural, 27
    used as adjectives (e.g., *vegetable soup*),
        28, 29
Noun clauses, 63
    defined, 63
    with *the fact that,* 65, 99
    with *it,* 65
    modals in, 68
    with question words, 64
    in reported speech, 67, 68
    subjunctive in, 68, 68*fn.*
    with *that,* 65, 68
    with *whether/if,* 64
    after *wish,* 107
    word order in, 64
Now that, 92, 98

O

Object(s):
    defined, 108
    of prepositions, 78, 82, 109
Object pronouns, 38, 41, 41*fn.,* 70
Of:
    in expressions of possession, 29
    in expressions of quantity, 32, 73
Once, 91
One:
    with count nouns, 29, 31, 32
    as impersonal pronoun, 41
One + singular noun, 32
One of, 32
One of + plural noun, 24, 32
Only after, 94*fn.*
Only if, 94, 98
Only in, 94*fn.*
Only when, 94*fn.*
On the other hand, 98, 102
Or, 88
Or else, 98, 103
Or not, 64
Other:
    expressions with, 43
    forms of, 42

Otherwise, 98, 103, 107
Ought to, 44
    degree of certainty in, 54
    in expressions of advisability, 46, 51
    in reported speech, 68
    summary chart of, 56

P

Paired conjunctions (e.g., *both … and*), 89, 89*fn.*
Parallel structure, 88, 89
Participial adjectives (e.g., *confusing* vs. *confused*),
    62
Participial phrases (SEE Modifying phrases)
Participles (SEE Modifying phrases; Past
    participle; Present participle)
Particles, defined, 75
Passive (form):
    by-phrase in, 58, 59, 60
    of causative verbs (e.g., *have it done*), 87
    defined, 58
    of gerunds (e.g., *being done*), 84, 85
    with *get* (e.g., *get worried*), 61
    of infinitives (e.g., *to be done*), 84, 85
    modals and phrasal modals in, 59
    non-progressive, (e.g., *the door is locked*), 60
    participial adjectives in (e.g., *amused*
        children), 62
    tense forms of, 58
Past habit, 51
Past participles, 7
    as adjective (e.g., *amused children*), 62
    irregular, 8–9
    in passive, 58, 59, 61
    (SEE ALSO *-Ed* forms)
Past progressive verbs, 5, 6
Past time (SEE Verb tenses)
Perfect/perfect progressive verbs
    (SEE Verb tenses)
Periods:
    British term for, 89*fn.*
    between independent clauses, 89
    in transitions, 99, 100
Personal names, contractions with, 12
Personal pronouns:
    agreement with nouns, 40
    contractions with, 11, 15
Phrasal modals:
    in conditional sentences, 104
    defined, 44
    after modals, 55
    passive form of, 59
Phrasal verbs, 75

Phrases:
  adjective, 74, 74*fn.*
  adverbial, 95–97
  defined, 63, 74
  gerund, 75
  prepositional, 109
Plan, 6
Plenty of, 31
Plural nouns, 22, 27 (SEE ALSO ***-S/-es***)
Polite requests, 17*fn.*, 49, 49*fn.*, 50
Possessive adjectives (*my, your,* etc.), 39,
  40, 87
Possessive nouns (e.g., *John's book*), 28, 29, 87
Possessive pronouns (*mine, yours,* etc.),
  39, 71
Preposition(s), 109–110
  in adjective clauses, 70, 71
  common combinations with adjectives and
    verbs, 110
  as connectives, 98, 100
  in expressions of cause and effect, 98, 99
  in expressions of condition, 98
  in expressions of contrast, 98, 102
  in expressions of possession, 29
  gerunds as objects of, 78, 82
  list of, 110
  after non-progressive passive verbs, 60
  punctuation with, 100
Prepositional phrases, 109
Present participles, 7
  as adjective (e.g., *amusing story*), 62
  irregular, 7
  special expressions followed by (e.g., *have fun
    doing*), 79
  spelling of *-ing* forms, 118
  with verbs of perception (e.g., *watch someone
    doing*), 86
  (SEE ALSO ***-Ing*** forms)
Present time (SEE Verb tenses)
Principal parts of verbs, 7
Progressive verbs, 1, 2, 3, 54
  in conditional sentences, 106
  vs. non-progressive, 3
  (SEE ALSO Verb tenses)
Pronouns:
  agreement with nouns, 40
  contractions with, 11, 15, 17, 116
  impersonal, 41
  indefinite, 40, 72
  object, 39, 41, 41*fn.*, 70
  personal, 11, 15, 40
  possessive, 39, 71

reflexive, 41
relative (SEE Adjective clauses)
subject, 39, 69, 74
Pronunciation:
  -ed, 122
  going to in informal speech, 17
  got to, 45
  had in reduced speech, 16
  have/has in reduced speech, 12
  ought to in informal speech, 46
  -s/-es, 22, 28, 122
  of tag questions, 115*fn.*
Punctuation:
  with adjective clauses, 73
  with adjective phrases, 74
  with adverb clauses, 90, 100
  with conjunctions, 88, 89, 100
  with independent clauses, 89
  in parallel structures, 88, 88*fn.*
  in quoted speech, 66
  in transitions, 99, 99*fn.*
  (SEE ALSO Apostrophes; Commas; Hyphen;
    Periods; Quotation marks; Semicolons)

Q

Quantity (SEE Expressions, of quantity)
Questions:
  information, 111
  negative, 114
  in quoted speech, 66
  tag, 115, 115*fn.*
  word order in, 111
  yes/no, 111, 114
Question words:
  contractions with, 116
  infinitives after, 65
  in noun clauses, 64
  with reduced *has/have,* 12
  summary of, 112–113
Quotation marks, 66, 66*fn.*
Quoted speech, 66
  vs. reported speech, 67

R

Raise/rise, 123
Recently, 11
Reduction:
  of adjective clauses, 74
  of adverb clauses, 95–97
Reflexive pronouns, 41
Regret, 77

Regular plural nouns, 27
Regular verbs, 4, 7
Remember/forget, 77
Repeated action in the past (*would, used to*), 51
Reported speech:
    defined, 67
    as indirect speech, 66*fn.*
    modals in, 68
    vs. quoted speech, 67
    verb tense in, 15, 16, 67
Restrictive adjective clauses, 73*fn.*

S

-S/-es, 22
    and adjectives, 108
    in count nouns, 29
    in plural nouns, 27
    in possessive nouns, 28
    pronunciation of, 22, 28, 122
    spelling with, 22
    in subject-verb agreement, 23, 25
    in verbs, 22
Say vs. *tell*, 67, 67*fn.*
-Self/-selves, 41
Semicolons, 89, 99*fn.*, 100, 100*fn.*
Sentences:
    complex (SEE Adjective clauses; Adverb
        clauses; Noun clauses)
    conditional (SEE Conditional sentences)
    imperative, 67
    interrogative (SEE Questions)
    inverted word order in, 94, 117
    negative, 117
    simple (SEE Subjects, verbs, objects)
Set/sit, 123
Several, 31, 32
Shall, 44, 50, 57
Should, 44
    in adverb clauses, 94
    in conditional sentences, 104, 106
    degree of certainty in, 54
    in expressions of advisability, 46, 51
    in expressions of expectations, 51
    in reported speech, 68
    with subjunctive verbs, 68, 68*fn.*
    summary chart of, 56
Simple form of a verb, 7
    with causative verbs, 87
    after *let* and *help*, 86
    with modal auxiliaries, 44
    in subjunctive, 68
    with verbs of perception, 86

Simple tenses, 1, 2, 4 (SEE ALSO Verb tenses)
Since:
    vs. *for*, 10, 14
    in adverb clauses, 91, 92, 98
    in adverbial phrases, 96
    duration of time, 10, 14, 91
    meaning *because*, 92
Singular/plural (SEE Agreement; Count/noncount
        nouns; Noun, regular and irregular plural;
        Noun, used as adjectives; *-S/-es*)
So, 98, 99
So long as, 91
Some, 29, 33
Some/any, 31
Some of, 24, 32
So that, 98, 101, 101*fn.*
So ... that, 100
Spelling:
    -ed/-ing, 118
    -s/-es, 22
Stative verbs (SEE Non-progressive verbs)
Stop, 75*fn.*, 77
Subject pronouns, 39, 69, 74
Subjects, verbs, objects, 108
Subject-verb agreement, 23
    with expressions of quantity, 24
    irregularities in, 25
    with *there + be*, 24
Subjunctive, in noun clauses, 68, 68*fn.*
Subordinate clauses (SEE Adjective clauses;
        Adverb clauses; Noun clauses)
Subordinating conjunctions, 90*fn.*
Such ... that/so ... that, 100
Suggest, 75*fn.*
Suppose, 47
Supposed to, 47, 51

T

Tag questions, 115, 115*fn.*
Tell vs. *say*, 67, 67*fn.*
Tenses (SEE Verb tenses)
Than, 55
That:
    in adjective clauses, 69, 70, 74
    in noun clauses, 65, 68
    in reported speech, 67
The:
    with definite nouns, 33, 35
    with generic nouns, 34, 36*fn.*
    guidelines for using, 36
    and subject-verb agreement, 25
    with titles and geographic names, 37

The number of, 24
There + be, 24
Therefore, 98, 99
They, 41, 115
Think about, 6
This/that, 36, 74, 102
Though, 92*fn.,* 98, 102, 102*fn.*
Till, 91
Time clauses, 91
    defined, 10, 19
    future, tense use in, 19
    as modifying adverbial phrases, 96
    with *since,* 10, 14, 91
    words used to introduce, 90, 91
Too:
    infinitives after, 84
Too/very, 84
Transitions:
    as connectives, 98, 100
    in expressions of cause and effect, 98, 99
    in expressions of condition, 98, 103
    in expressions of contrast, 98, 102
    punctuation with, 100
Transitive/intransitive verbs:
    defined, 58, 108
    in passive form, 58
    troublesome (e.g., *lay/lie*), 123
Try, 77

U

Uncountable nouns (SEE Noncount nouns)
Unless, 94, 98
Until, 91
Upon, 96*fn.*
Upon + -ing, 97
Used to, 51, 57, 78

V

Verbals (SEE Gerunds; Infinitives, common verbs
    followed by)
Verbs:
    causative, 87
    defined, 108
    with final *-s/-es,* 22
    irregular, 4, 7, 8–9
    linking, 123
    non-progressive, 3
    of perception, 86
    phrasal, 75
    progressive, 1, 2, 3, 54, 106
    regular, 4, 7

    subjunctive, 68
    transitive and intransitive, 58, 108, 123
Verb tenses:
    continuous, 119*fn.*
    future perfect, 20
    future perfect progressive, 20
    future progressive, 20
    in passive, 58, 59, 60, 61
    past perfect, 15
    past perfect progressive, 16
    past progressive, 5, 6
    present perfect, 10, 11, 13, 19
    present perfect progressive, 14
    present progressive, 1, 2, 3, 19
    in reported speech, 15, 16, 67
    simple future, 17
    simple past, 4, 5, 7, 13
    simple present, 1, 2, 19
    summary of, 119–121
    with *wish,* 107
Very, 84
Very + few/little, 31
Voiced and voiceless sounds, 122

W

Was/were, 4, 105, 106
Was/were able to, 52
Was/were going to, 6, 68, 107
What, 113
*What + * a form of *do,* 113
What kind of, 113
When, 5
    in adjective clauses, 71
    in adverb clauses, 91
    in adverbial phrases, 96
    meaning *upon,* 96*fn.*
    in questions, 112
Whenever, 91
Where:
    in adjective clauses, 71
    in questions, 112
Whereas, 92*fn.*
Whether, 64
Whether or not, 93, 98
Which:
    in adjective clauses, 69, 69*fn.,* 70, 72*fn.,* 74
    in questions, 113
While:
    in adverb clauses, 91, 92, 98, 102, 102*fn.*
    in adverbial phrases, 96, 97
    vs. *whereas,* 92*fn.*

Whose, 71, 112
Who/whom:
    in adjective clauses, 69, 70
    in questions, 112
    vs. *whose,* 71
Why, 112
Why don't, 50
Will, 44
    vs. *be going to,* 18
    in conditional sentences, 104
    contractions with, 116
    degree of certainty in, 54
    future, 17, 20
    negative, 17
    in polite requests, 17*fn.,* 49
    after *so that,* 101
    summary chart of, 56
Wish, 107
Word order:
    in adjective phrases, 74*fn.*
    after negatives, 117
    in noun clauses, 64
    after *only if,* 94
    in questions, 111

Would, 44
    in conditional sentences, 104, 105
    contractions with, 116
    to express repeated action in past, 51
    in polite requests, 49
    in reported speech, 68
    after *so that,* 101
    in suggestions/advice, 46*fn.*
    summary chart of, 57
    with *wish,* 107
Would have, 104, 105*fn.,* 107*fn.*
Would rather, 55
Would you mind, 50, 50*fn.*

Y

-Y, final, spelling:
    with *-ed, -ing,* 118
    with *-s/-es,* 22
Yes/no questions, 111, 114
Yet, 98, 102
You:
    as impersonal pronoun, 41